GET
HEARD
GET
RESULTS

GET HEARD GET RESULTS

How to Get Buy-In for Your Ideas and Initiatives

SIMON DOWLING

WILEY

First published as *Work with me* in 2016 by John Wiley & Sons Australia, Ltd

42 McDougall St, Milton Qld 4064

Office also in Melbourne

This edition first published in 2020 by John Wiley & Sons Australia, Ltd

Typeset in 12.5/14.5pt Arno Pro

© 2engage Pty Ltd 2016

The moral rights of the author have been asserted

ISBN: 978-0-730-38201-0

A catalogue record for this book is available from the National Library of Australia

Cover design by Wiley

Internal artwork by Linden Duck

Printed in the USA by Quad/Graphics

V09948F11-6F65-45ED-91AA-827266B28FB9_103019

Disclaimer

The material in this publication is of the nature of general comment only, and does not represent professional advice. It is not intended to provide specific guidance for particular circumstances and it should not be relied on as the basis for any decision to take action or not take action on any matter which it covers. Readers should obtain professional advice where appropriate, before making any such decision. To the maximum extent permitted by law, the author and publisher disclaim all responsibility and liability to any person, arising directly or indirectly from any person taking or not taking action based on the information in this publication.

Contents

About the author

Simon Dowling is a leading thinker on creating teams and workplaces that thrive on collaboration.

His passion for team dynamics started when he led a double life: during the day he was a commercial lawyer in a big city firm and at night he was a performer in improvised comedy shows, including the hit TV show *Thank God You're Here*. The contrast between these two worlds was what spurred him to go it alone in his own practice so he could help others pair the technical skills of negotiating agreement with a sense of play, engagement and, most importantly, action!

Based in Melbourne, Australia, Simon now works with senior leaders and their teams as a mentor and coach, and is a highly sought-after conference speaker. His clients are like a variety show bag, ranging from funky start-ups and tech companies to banks, government agencies, educational institutions and elite sporting clubs.

Simon continues to admire the way a great improvisation company can come together and create compelling scenes and stories for its audiences without a hint of a script — the essence of true collaboration.

When not working with people or presenting at conferences, Simon can be found hanging out at one of Melbourne's many cafés and coffee hotspots, or at the beach with his family, assessing the surf conditions (waiting for the perfect wave, of course).

simondowling.com.au

Acknowledgements

Writing this book has been an incredible privilege. In truth, it couldn't have happened without the support of a whole army of wonderful people. I'd like to take a moment to thank them.

I start with my amazing wife, Amanda. Amanda's the one who gave me her buy-in (at so many levels) and who held the fort while I bunkered down to write. She's been my number one cheer squad throughout the project, and I will always be hers. Our two amazing kids — Sophie and Samuel — were so patient as Dad spent most of the summer holidays obsessing with his book, even when the beach seemed like a much better idea. Thanks guys, I love you heaps.

Thank you to all my family and friends. Aside from all those supportive 'how's your book going?' conversations, you might be surprised how often I've pictured you as I rewrote a vexing paragraph or sentence. Having you in my mind helped me to say what I wanted to say.

A huge thanks to those who challenged me to write this in the first place, and pushed me to — and then through — a place of doubt and discomfort. Matt Church, Peter Cook and Lynne Cazaly were all instrumental in helping me to just write the freakin' thing. Thanks also to David Simpson, who helped me keep a detached calmness as I entered the fray.

I also want to acknowledge those who played an important role in shaping my thinking on the topic of this book, even though it was many years ago now. Thank you to Eliezer Kornhauser, Jonny Schauder, Sandy Caspi Sable and Shawn Whelan for the many hours of debate and discussion.

Finally, I've been blessed to have an amazing team of people working with me on this project: Kelly Irving, my editor extraordinaire; Linden Duck for his cool sketches; Nicole Bailey and Amy Rockman for their incredible support at HQ; the guys at Glovers Station who ensured my coffee cup runneth over; and of course the dedicated team at Wiley — Lucy Raymond, Chris Shorten, Jem Bates, Ingrid Bond, Theo Vassili and all those behind the scenes. To you all I say, thank you!

Foreword

You get really good at what you do. Your skills and background knowledge and experience make your work valuable. Your input sought. You hit your stride.

Then you get promoted to 'leadership.' Suddenly you're not in control of everything anymore. You're overwhelmed. You try to do as much as you can yourself. But now you're the bottleneck. You delegate to others and try to 'mentor' them and you are accused of micro-managing. You try leaving them alone, and they complain you need to show more leadership. To top it all off, you get put in charge of a change effort and six months in, nobody's changing.

It's a paradox at the heart of leadership, of negotiation, of getting things done: sometimes getting traction requires treading more lightly. We have to let go of *getting* people on board, and instead invite them aboard.

Simon offers us the essential ingredients — mindsets and skills for how to invite people on board, whether it's your spouse, your kids, your colleagues or your clients. In clear, engaging terms he points out the assumptions that can get us stuck, the common mistakes we all make, and a handful of practical techniques for engaging others' interest, passion, and commitment.

He had me on board from the first page. And long after the last page he has me using his advice. That's the highest compliment I can give a book.

Sheila Heen
Co-author of *Thanks for the Feedback* and *Difficult Conversations*
Cambridge, Massachusetts

Prologue

Go to the people. Live with them. Learn from them. Love them. Start with what they know. Build with what they have. But with the best leaders, when the work is done, the task accomplished, the people will say 'We have done this ourselves.'
Lao Tzu, the founder of Taoism

Imagine if each of your ideas, initiatives or projects was a book on a shelf in a bookstore. Would anyone pick it up? Would they fork out the cash to purchase a copy? Would they even read it? More importantly would they act on the things they'd learned there? Would they take it back to their teams, colleagues and friends, and start a conversation about it? Would they put it on their own bookshelf or post selfies on Instagram of them reading it? Would they buy extra copies to give to their friends? Would people bang on your door, asking to work with you on writing the sequel?

We've all got ideas we want others to buy into.

Whether it's a new initiative, a project or even a way of life, we want people to jump on board and support us wholeheartedly and see our idea through to fruition. We need other people's cooperation, their commitment and their energy. We need them to smile, jump in and ask, 'Where do I sign up?' This infectious enthusiasm and dedication to see the job through to the end is exactly what we need to effect change.

This is a book about building cooperation and buy-in. Buy-in is the thing that makes and drives highly engaged, creative and motivated teams. As you've no doubt experienced before, without buy-in, projects and ideas falter or fail to even get off the ground. Without buy-in, your ideas will come crashing down around you. Exorbitant costs, wasted money, squandered time and resources are all dangerous consequences of the inability to build buy-in effectively. Without buy-in, managers are forced to crack whips or find ever juicier carrots to dangle in front of their team to get them to take action.

So how do you get others to buy into your ideas — to work with you?

Over the past couple of decades, I've had the good fortune to work with people from a wide variety of backgrounds — entrepreneurs, senior executives, charity workers, tech geeks, elite sporting teams, government officials, lawyers, health professionals and salespeople. One thing that's clear to me is that although everyone's situation, ideas and context will differ, the challenge of building buy-in is not a technical one; it's a human one. *How do I connect with this person? How do I help them to see things differently? How can I make sense of their concerns? How do I foster a sense of trust? What can I do to convince them to take action?*

Answering these kinds of questions comes more naturally to some people than to others. After all, each of us has been forging our own approach since we first tried to convince the other kids in the schoolyard to trade football cards with us.

What many of us *don't* get is an opportunity to formally learn the skills required to build cooperation and buy-in. Skills such as influencing, negotiating, persuading, collaborating and problem solving. As we build up our pool of technical knowledge — in whatever domain that may be — there is a presumption that we've got the rest covered. But that ain't necessarily so. These are skills that need to be learned.

This book will show you how to get heard and get results, not through coercion or manipulation, but through the gentle art of buy-in. It will equip you with the skills to:

» become a true catalyst of change

» foster the mindset of a champion of buy-in

» build relationships of trust that will underpin your quest for buy-in

» set the mood and create an emotional *bias to yes* in your target audience

» overcome objections and resistance

» build genuine agreement and commitment

» convert buy-in into meaningful long-term change.

I'm a practical guy, so this book has lots of practical ideas and exercises at the end of each chapter so you can stop and apply what you're learning in the real world.

Each chapter builds on the ones before it, so I recommend you work your way through them in sequence. My hope is that you return to chapters that interest you or, when you're stuck, for inspiration and help at any point on the buy-in journey.

I wrote this book because I'm a big believer in what can be achieved when you spark the energy of others. It's in this way that I hope to spark yours. By the time you reach the end of the book, you should feel a renewed sense of confidence and the courage to be a true champion of buy-in. To be someone who takes their power not from their position or authority, but from their ability to engage others and generate true, authentic buy-in. If you ask me, we need more people like that in the world.

So what do you say — *are you in?*

Part I
Get Ready

The path to buy-in begins well before you sit down at the proverbial table and pitch your idea. First, there's important work to be done: both on yourself, and on understanding the bigger picture. Before we can 'Go!', we need to 'Get Ready'.

Abraham Lincoln once famously stated, 'Give me six hours to chop down a tree and I will spend the first four sharpening the axe.'

Let's get sharpening ... Chapter 1

CHAPTER 1
SHIFT
Choose the power of buy-in

Let's be the first to send a man to the moon.

Let's make cameras digital.

Let's set up a network of private drivers who'll take people wherever they want to go.

We need $250 000 and four new staff to upgrade our customer database system.

We should trial driverless cars.

I need management to support a 5 per cent pay rise for my team next year.

Darling, I'd really like to have another child.

Let's make another Police Academy movie!

Every one of these ideas needed the instigator to bring other people willingly and enthusiastically on board to breathe life into it. Each required some careful persuasion, a lot of negotiation and probably some persistent nagging, but the outcome couldn't be a reluctant 'All right, do what you want'. To be successful, the outcome had to be 'I'm with you on this ... Let's do it ... Sign me up'. Head and heart had to be on board and action had to follow closely behind.

In your own organisation, you probably hear comments like these every day:

» 'I know what it will take to improve team performance.'

» 'I know how to improve our product so we'll get fewer customer complaints.'

» 'We know what our new strategic direction needs to look like.'

» 'I know how marketing can better support us in the field.'

» 'I know what we need to do to stop losing market share.'

» 'We know why morale is low and what to do about it.'

» 'I know how to make sure everyone puts their cup in the dishwasher.'

Yet how many of these 'I know' statements make it from idea to implementation? Too often they are accompanied by an exasperated 'If only I could get others to think or feel the same way'.

A GREAT IDEA WILL STAY JUST THAT – AN IDEA – UNLESS YOU CAN GET OTHERS TO WORK WITH YOU TO TURN IT INTO A REALITY.

This is especially true in the context of the modern organisation, where your idea is competing for attention with hundreds, perhaps thousands, of others.

Politicians need us to buy into their policies and vision in the same way that senior executives need their shareholders to buy into the vision of their organisation. Managers need the buy-in of their teams, while team members need the buy-in of people across the business to implement new ideas and projects. The implications of getting this wrong are too great to ignore.

The cost of getting it wrong

In his book *Leading Change*, renowned thought leader John Kotter reports that 70 per cent of change initiatives fail. That's a lot of wasted money, time, energy and resources — not to mention the sheer frustration! One reason for this type of failure is a lack of buy-in from the people needed to bring that change to life.

In 2005 Australian airline Qantas learned this the hard way when its leadership team announced it was introducing a new parts management system called *Jetsmart*. Things did not go smoothly for the senior leaders, who were heavily criticised for failing to engage with engineers, operational staff and unions. As a result, Jetsmart (nicknamed 'Dumbjet' by Qantas engineers) became mired in endless disputes and problems, all of which took place in the public spotlight. Three years and $40 million later, Qantas announced that it would retire Jetsmart and start over.[1]

The costs associated with a lack of buy-in from the right people can be huge.

Here are some more examples to get you thinking:

» The product development team in a company I was working with had created a very nifty piece of software designed to help its customers manage their account with the company. The software promised to make customers' lives easier and to help retain customers. Yet the only way to get customers to use the software was for the sales team to introduce them to it. Despite promises to the contrary, the folks in sales simply weren't signing customers up for the tool. The software sat on a shelf gathering dust, while tensions between product developers and the sales team quickly escalated.

» A professional services firm, another of my clients, once announced a series of workshops for its staff designed to equip people with the skills to improve their productivity. The only problem was, no one enrolled. After some investigation, initially aimed at finding more suitable dates, it became clear that the people who had purchased the workshops hadn't done enough to get buy-in from the different parts of the business. In fact, it turned out that the announcement to run the program had been taken as an insult by many of the managers, who felt they were being told they weren't productive enough!

» Craig, a software engineer new to his company, wanted to shift his team to a new project management methodology. Against the backdrop of a fast-changing industry, Craig saw it as critical that project teams worked at a much faster pace, trying new things and finding ways to experiment with new approaches. Craig had experienced the benefits of the change first-hand in his previous job, and thought it was a no-brainer. But several months later, Craig found his efforts stalling in the face of a lack of buy-in from his leadership team and also from many long-standing staff, who couldn't see how the change would be good for them. Craig's frustration led him to leave the company less than twelve months after starting there.

Do these scenarios sound familiar? Have you experienced something similar in your own world?

In each of the above examples, what started out as an idea, ripe with potential, ended up becoming a problem that failed to achieve buy-in. And the cost? Large amounts of money being spent trying to bring projects to life that were doomed to failure — or to rescue them from the clutches of defeat. Add to that the lost value of the failed opportunity, and you already have a pretty hefty price tag.

The costs continue to add up, including the strain on people's time, energy and relationships, as they battle into various stages of resistance. This dampens everyone's morale and causes disengagement, resulting in a learned helplessness that eventually has people shrugging their shoulders and saying, 'What's the point? No one will listen, so I may as well just stop trying.' People disengage, resign or — worse still — hang around giving off one hell of a bad vibe.

Change doesn't happen in the executive boardroom, as all of these examples show. It happens on the frontline of an organisation and involves a number of people, from board members to employees. Without buy-in from all of those involved, you're hammering a round peg into a square hole.

What is buy-in really?

For those who can win buy-in to their ideas and initiatives, the world is their proverbial oyster. But to understand how to build buy-in you first have to look at what buy-in is and what it is not.

The online *Cambridge English Dictionary* defines buy-in as 'the fact of agreeing and accepting something that someone suggests'. But that's not enough.

> *TRUE* BUY-IN REQUIRES WILLING AND ENTHUSIASTIC COMMITMENT. CREATING BUY-IN IS ABOUT BUILDING A GENUINELY VOLUNTARY CHOICE, GETTING PEOPLE TO THE PLACE WHERE THEY SAY 'YES!' NOT BECAUSE THEY *HAVE TO*, BUT BECAUSE THEY *WANT TO*.

Real buy-in goes much further than achieving compliance or conformity. It's the ultimate form of influence. It creates intellectual and emotional alignment between two or more people. It wins a share of someone's devotion, of their passion and energy. If you want others' creativity, engagement, participation, advocacy and championship then you need to affect them under the surface, through their skin.

To get to this holy place, there can be no tricks of the mind, no manipulation, no threats, no forced hands and no hypnosis. These moves may sometimes work to influence people to act in the way you want them to act, but if it's genuine buy-in you seek, then people will subscribe to that only when they *choose* to and feel it's safe to do so.

Here's a simple example we can all relate to (whether parents or not):

Dad: Sam, have you cleaned up your room yet?

Sam: Yes.

Dad: [After a quick look into his room] That's not clean, Sam. Please go and tidy up your room as I asked.

Sam: After.

Dad: No, now please. [Sam does nothing.] Sam, you've got five seconds to go in there and start cleaning up your room or you won't be going to the park with us after lunch. Five ... four ... three ... two ... [Sam runs to his room.]

Do you think Dad is winning? Perhaps. Until a few minutes later, when he walks into Sam's room to discover him sitting on the floor playing with his toys.

Dad: Sam, that's not tidying up! You're playing! That's it, no park for you!

Sam starts crying.

Consider what happens when Mum enters the room.

Mum: Sam, why do you think Daddy wants you to tidy up your room?

Sam: Because he's bossy.

Mum: Yes, Daddy is bossy sometimes. But I don't think that's why he wants you to tidy up. Can you think why he thinks it's so important?

Sam: So I don't step on my toys and break them?

Mum: That's a great reason. Do you think that's important?

Sam: Yes, but Mum I don't like tidying up.

Mum: Me neither. But if we do it fast then maybe we can go to the park sooner. What do you reckon, should we see how fast you can tidy it up and how quickly we can get to the park?

Sam: Okay. Can we take the soccer ball?

Mum: That's a great idea. Let's get that room done first, shall we?

Sam: I'm going to be fast... like the Flash...

In this scenario, Dad could easily be a manager, and Sam his team member. Dad attempts to get heard by relying on his authority, his implicit right to call the shots, but let's call a spade a spade: it's coercion. Sam's not impressed.

Mum, however, creates a new perspective. She seeks not just to be heard, but to get Sam's *buy-in*. Mum has not only secured Sam's cooperation this time, but it's likely she will be successful in getting Sam to tidy his room next time as well.

When I share this example in my workshops, my participants usually exclaim how patient Mum is. Spot on. It's a big reason that she succeeds. When you're asking someone not just to hear and understand an idea, but to understand *why* the idea matters and to decide *if* they are willing to buy into that idea — that takes time and patience.

From 'decree' to 'win me' — a fundamental shift

'Buy-in is critical to success. Organisations only succeed when many people are pulling together to achieve a common goal. Having buy-in materially impacts the success of the organisation's ability to achieve this.'

Ronnie Fink, Corporate Development Director, SEEK Limited

In the context of the workplace, the most traditional source of power is hierarchy and vested authority. The closer you are to the top of the tree, the more you get to call the shots. This gives rise to what I call *influence by decree*. In other words, if you have a stick that's big enough and threatening enough, you can wave it at people and say, 'Do what I am asking you to do. Listen to what I am saying … or else.'

Influence by decree has been common in organisations and institutions for a long time. It was an old favourite of folks like Alexander the Great and Henry VIII (not exactly contemporary role models of leadership).

Influence by decree is a mainstay of more traditional industries — those that are best represented by a factory model. The worker in that context is part of a large 'machine' that focuses on repeating processes to generate more product. In that world, entrepreneurship and creativity are the reserve of a select few, perhaps the owner of the business and those who sit around the executive table. For the rest, the message is simple: do your job, or we'll find someone who can.

Of course, this model is still alive and strong in some organisations — and it probably always will be. But we're now living in an age when newer industries, those fuelled by ideas and creativity, have begun to dominate — information services, communication and media, research and development, consultancy and design.[2] This is an era when ideas represent the greatest form of currency. When organisations that truly thrive know how not just to create the ideas, but also to bring them to life — fast.

THE AGE OF BUY-IN

Any enterprise serious about keeping pace with a market that's evolving faster than ever — whether through innovation, speed-to-market or customer responsiveness — must create an environment where ideas can truly thrive. They must let go of slow and cumbersome models of getting things done born in the industrial age. Managers must loosen the reins and ask people to think for themselves, to generate ideas and find ways of bringing them to life, without waiting for someone with more authority to tell them what to do.

EXIT *DECREE*; ENTER THE WORLD OF *WIN ME*, WHERE PEOPLE COLLABORATE ACROSS TEAMS AND INFLUENCE WITHOUT AUTHORITY. WELCOME TO THE AGE OF BUY-IN.

Aside from its strategic importance, the emphasis on generating buy-in is something employees expect. Companies are asking more than ever of their people: more of their creative genius, more hours, more ownership, more initiative, more flexibility, more tolerance of ambiguity, change and chaos. In return, employees in this creative economy need and expect more — and that doesn't just mean money. It means more autonomy and more freedom.

People who give more expect to have a voice. They expect to be heard and to be able to shape decisions about their work. They expect leaders to earn their support, not take it as a given.

We want to work in organisations that match our own values; we want to be part of, and to initiate, company projects and initiatives.

David Noël, former Head of Internal Communications at SoundCloud, summed it up perfectly when he said, 'We're seeing a generation of people who are making decisions about where to work based on how their personal values map to company values. Today, more than twice as many employees are motivated by work passion than career ambition.'[3]

Easy to say, but what to do?

It's one thing to talk about the importance of getting people's buy-in. It's another thing to achieve it.

When you seek others' cooperation in a busy organisation without relying on a mandate from management, all kinds of interesting tensions arise. In my own work, I regularly come across managers who are struggling to let go and give their team members the space to experiment, create and even (gasp!) fail.

Often, these practices are at odds with the diet of management on which they themselves have been raised. It makes them feel uncomfortable. It seems chaotic and risky. At the same time, managers still need to manage, so how do they do that without managing by decree?

Some teams also struggle to embrace the degree of autonomy and entrepreneurship that is offered to them. Suddenly faced with a multitude of people they need to work with, and without a clear instruction manual from management, their mindset and skills are put to the test. *How do I cope with this freedom to create results, to develop and deliver strategies and to be accountable for the choices I've made? Do I know how to make those kinds of decisions? Do I know how to get others on board and eager to cooperate with me?*

This is where teams and organisations can easily fall over: by failing to create a culture where people are able influence and lead others, even when they're not in a position of authority, and by failing to equip them with the skills and understanding to do so.

Well, there's a new kind of power in town. It's the power that comes to those who are able to cut through all of these challenges — by engaging others and building buy-in.

A GENTLE ART

Yes, building buy-in is a skill that comes more naturally to some than to others, but the good news is it can be learned and mastered by *anyone*.

> ### TOP TIP
>
> To master the gentle art of buy-in, you need a blend of the right skills, attributes and mindset. I use the term 'gentle art' because it requires patience, empathy and careful thinking. You need to know when to yield control in order to maintain it. You need a healthy dose of emotional intelligence. You need to be willing to go slow to go fast.

Of course, having a good idea to begin with is always going to interest and excite those you're seeking buy-in from, but even the best ideas in the world can languish in the hands of someone who doesn't know how to engage and influence others — or worse, someone who simply puts people off.

Equally, buy-in shouldn't equate to paralysis. Many of us have worked in a team or a company where there was so much consultation and committee-style decision making that nothing ever happened. Where that's the case, your relationship with the idea of building buy-in might be a tad … strained.

YOU NEED TO KNOW WHEN BUY-IN IS A FUNCTION OF GENTLE PERSUASION AND DIALOGUE, AND WHEN IT'S A FUNCTION OF GETTING YOUR TRAIN MOVING AND ASKING OTHERS TO JUMP ON BOARD.

That's why you have to learn to be a *champion of buy-in*.

Over to you

1. Think of one 'decree' and one 'win me' situation you've been in before.

2. How did the two situations differ?

3. How enthusiastic were you and were others during the buy-in process?

4. How did this affect the end result?

* * *

So far we've explored why buy-in matters. There are serious costs to getting it wrong, but also many opportunities for those who get it right, especially for businesses in the creative economy of ideas. So what does it mean to pursue 'win me' rather than influence by 'decree'? What are the choices you're really making? These are the questions we'll investigate in chapter 2.

CHAPTER 2
MINDSET
Imagine what's possible

'The only person you are destined to become is the person you decide to be.'
Ralph Waldo Emerson

How do you feel about the idea of buy-in as a preferred way of getting heard and getting results? Does it make perfect sense? Or does it seem more natural to you to just do what the boss says? Perhaps there's a little (or not so little) voice in your head that's saying, *Sure, but how good would it be if I could just tell everyone what to do! Life would be just so much easier …*

The culture you've grown up in has a big part to play in whether you relate more to the 'decree' (top-down) or 'win me' (collaborative) approach we discussed in the previous chapter. For example, certain countries operate to a very formal, hierarchical norm, while others have a far more informal, egalitarian norm.[4] Cultural norms can also come from your family upbringing, not to mention your previous workplaces and their organisational cultures. All of these experiences are likely to shape your assumptions about the roles of authority and autonomy in the workplace.

In table 2.1 we take a closer look at the differences between the two approaches.

Table 2.1: 'decree' versus 'win me'

Approach	'Decree'		'Win me!'
Purpose	Ensure compliance	vs	Generate buy-in
Outcome	People do things because they *have* to	vs	People do things because they *want* to
Sources of power	Hierarchy, authority, carrots and sticks	vs	The merit of your ideas Your personal ability to build trust and generate buy-in
Primary modes of engagement	Telling, directing, explaining, persuading, rewarding, punishing	vs	Negotiating, consulting, joint problem-solving
Likely result	When people are merely compliant, they are more likely to: » take action for as long as any carrots or sticks have effect » freeze or give up in the face of obstacles	vs	When people buy into an idea, they are more likely to: » take ownership of the idea or initiative » take longer to begin taking action

Approach	'Decree'		'Win me!'
	» look to you for guidance at each step of the way » need constant monitoring to ensure sustained action » grumble.		» question and challenge » find a way to overcome obstacles » take action over the long term » come up with a way forward that's different from what you'd originally planned.

In truth, there is a place for both approaches. You may find that you swing between the two in different situations and with different audiences. There will be times when you're in a position of authority (as a manager or a parent, for example) and you need to make a decision and move on it quickly. But this can also come at a cost.

Remember the Qantas example in chapter 1? The chief financial officer of Qantas at the time, Peter Gregg, is on record as having said, 'We wouldn't ask the engineers what their views on our software systems were. We'll put in what we think is appropriate for us.'[5] A very bold moment of decree, which turned out not to be such a good call.

Your assumptions about which of the two approaches is 'normal' will shape the way you respond to, and apply, what you learn in each chapter in this book. If your natural style is to give people autonomy, then much of this book will feel in sync with that. If, on the other hand, your natural or ingrained style is to operate according to hierarchy and authority, then some of what you'll soon learn will likely feel challenging. But don't worry — this book has been designed to help you with that!

Whatever your default style, you have to *choose* your approach from one situation to the next. You can't have a both-ways bet by hovering somewhere between 'decree' and 'win me'. By trying to keep one foot in the 'decree' camp, you risk undermining all your hard work. The moment people sense that you're about to spring into authoritarian mode, they're likely to scurry back into their holes like sandcrabs on a beach.

EVERY TIME YOU SEEK TO INFLUENCE OTHERS TO TAKE ACTION AROUND AN IDEA OR INITIATIVE, YOU HAVE TO *CHOOSE* TO INFLUENCE THEM THROUGH THE 'WIN ME' APPROACH. YOU HAVE TO CHOOSE TO BE COLLABORATIVE. YOU HAVE TO CHOOSE TO BE A CHAMPION OF BUY-IN.

Those who consistently choose 'win me' over 'decree' are what I call *champions of buy-in*.

Champions of buy-in choose a 'win me' approach because they understand the benefits to be gained from creating true buy-in. They also understand the costs of getting it wrong.

Champions of buy-in know that the role of 'win me' is much bigger than simply getting the best outcome on a project or initiative. They believe that buy-in is critical to creating highly engaged, motivated teams — that by fostering people's sense of autonomy, they are promoting a creative and robust exchange of ideas.

In fact, champions of buy-in are building a *culture* of buy-in. They shape an organisation so that people from all levels can reach out to others, connect with them and enlist their cooperation around important ideas and projects — not because they have to, but because they want to.

THIS IS A CULTURE WHERE 'GETTING HEARD' IS NOT ABOUT BEING THE LOUDEST OR MOST SENIOR VOICE IN THE ROOM, BUT A FOCUS ON ENGAGING OTHERS IN A SHARED INTENT, A CULTURE WHERE THE FOCUS ON CREATING BUY-IN IS THE NORM.

Of course, champions of buy-in aren't naive. They know that decree is not a dirty word. They know that there will always be a time and place for telling, directing and explaining. Organisations or leaders who don't know when and where that is can often become mired in indecision and endless consultation when the time for action has long passed.

So what does it take to be a champion of buy-in?

A champion mindset

We all possess a set of beliefs and a way of thinking that underpins the way we approach everything we do — we call this our mindset. Mindset defines your personal parameters of 'what's possible'. Mindset defines what's worthwhile. Mindset defines your care factor. As Henry Ford once famously said, 'Whether you believe you can do a thing or not, you are right.'

As you make your way through the next few chapters, every idea I share with you will test your ability to:

» take on the perspective of others

» respect the opinions of others and appreciate that buy-in is an entirely subjective question

» be patient and willing to explore different ways of getting to the same outcome

» be a problem solver, not a 'my way or the highway' kind of person

» listen and understand others

» accept that you rarely get to a desired outcome by following a straight path.

All of these ask you to adopt a particular stance: a *what's possible?* stance.

What's possible?

What's possible? is an attitude of curiosity, creativity and commitment to the best possible outcome — not simply the outcome you already have in mind. When you ask *what's possible?*, you remain flexible, adaptive, creative and curious as you enter the unpredictable terrain of building people's support and cooperation around your ideas.

Start by reflecting on *what's possible?* rather than presuming the way forward is obvious:

» 'I wonder what people need in order for this to work …'

» 'I wonder what I can learn from other people's experiences in similar situations.'

» 'I wonder what needs to be done to make this proposal attractive to others.'

» 'I wonder what I can do to help other people engage with this idea.'

» 'I wonder what the best outcome could actually look like.'

» 'I wonder what would happen if I myself looked at this whole thing in a different way.'

It can be hard to maintain *what's possible?* in a world where it often feels as though you have to prove yourself every day by demonstrating your expertise and credentials. As Japanese Buddhist monk Shunryu Suzuki so elegantly put it, 'In the beginner's mind there are many possibilities, in the expert's mind there are few.' Remaining curious and open requires us to train our minds to have the courage to accept that we don't have all the answers all the time. (I say courage here because I think this is the ultimate form of confidence — allowing others to see you for what you don't know, just as much as for what you do know.)

CHAMPIONS OF BUY-IN ARE WILLING TO SIT IN THE DISCOMFORT OF NOT KNOWING. THEY ARE COMFORTABLE WITH SILENCES, PAUSES, QUESTIONS FOR WHICH THERE ARE NO OBVIOUS ANSWERS, LISTENING TO OTHERS VOICE THEIR CONCERNS AND OBJECTIONS WITHOUT FEELING THE NEED TO SHUT THEM DOWN.

What's possible? is a function of two key mindsets (see figure 2.1):

1. an inclusive mindset
2. an abundance mindset.

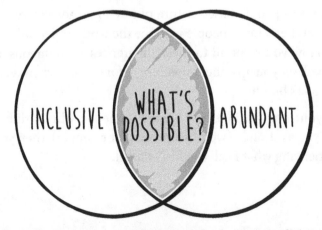

Figure 2.1: the two key mindsets of *what's possible?*

Let's now explore what each of these mindsets involves.

An inclusive mindset

There's a scene in the original *Men in Black* movie where Will Smith's character is going through the recruitment process for the MIB squad, covert agents tasked with identifying and managing aliens on Earth. Smith's character is standing in a room alongside a group of other highly polished looking candidates, all of whom are in military gear.

Suddenly, amidst howling sirens and flashing lights, two-dimensional targets of aliens start to pop up. The men are being tested. Who can most swiftly and successfully 'neutralise' all threats? As the trigger-happy recruits systematically blast bullet holes in the alien-looking targets springing up around them, Smith refrains — until taking careful aim and firing a single shot at one target: it's of a young girl with blond pigtails, holding schoolbooks and smiling sweetly.

It turns out, of course, she's the only target that actually represents a threat. Smith's inclusive mindset enabled him to look past the obvious differences and make a more astute, intuitive assessment of the situation.

The very people-based nature of buy-in means you're going to encounter a lot of people who see the world differently from you. How you respond to these differences at an unconscious level will set you up either for failure or for success when seeking someone's buy-in.

If your first instinct is to regard someone who is different from you as strange (weirdly dressed, for example), then you're experiencing what I call an *alien mindset*.

Top tip

Remember, difference is part and parcel of working in a team. The final outcome of any project or idea needs to account for all the differences in order for it to succeed. Therefore, you must learn to identify and embrace difference rather than waiting to be ambushed by it. To be successful at buy-in, you must learn to foster and maintain an *inclusive mindset*, which means seeing anyone who is different from you as a potential ally rather than an alien.

ALIEN ATTACK!

Let's be clear: an alien mindset does not make you a bad person. Everyone's alien mindset gets triggered from time to time, from context to context. If somewhere in my history I have learned to be suspicious of skinheads with tattoos, then it will take conscious, rational thinking on my part to challenge that kind of prejudice.

An alien mindset often kicks in when you're feeling isolated or 'ganged up on'. Let's look at this example of Trudy, a young manager I once worked with who was leading a major change in her workplace.

Trudy had tried her hardest to engage the leadership team in the change she was implementing. She had run sessions to take them through the proposed changes and their rationale, but she was still being met with resistance. When I asked her how she thought the process had gone so far, she took a deep breath, let out a sigh and shook her head

(Continued)

slightly. 'The more I put my vision out there, the more people want to question it. Everyone's a genius! They all think they know best. But they can't all run the show! These people are more interested in grandstanding in front of the CEO than actually listening to a decent proposal.'

Trudy realised how her alien mindset was causing her to be defensive. She decided to let the 'us versus them' dynamic go, coaching herself to echo new, inclusive thoughts in her mind until they started to dominate her thinking. To help her to avoid slipping back into old thought patterns, she asked a colleague to challenge her any time he heard her say something that suggested an alien mindset. Gradually, Trudy felt less emotional at moments of pushback and began to see that this behaviour was less about her and more about them. In fact, she became curious about what was driving her team to behave that way, which led her to understand them instead of dismissing them.

Being inclusive isn't just something you can turn on at the flick of a psychological switch. Your mindset is the sum of your thoughts, your deeply ingrained assumptions about people and the way the world works. Those things don't change simply because you want them to. It's something you've got to work at by making conscious choices about the way you will react in the face of difference and disagreement. Those conscious choices start out as little seedlings that you plant into your conscious mind, tending to them each day until they take root in the subconscious, as you persistently 'weed out' the deeply ingrained assumptions when they resurface.

Table 2.2 demonstrates the responses you can choose to adopt to shift an alien mindset into an inclusive one.

Table 2.2: an alien vs inclusive response

Your alien response	Your inclusive response
» No one's listening to me.	» Have I done enough listening myself?
» They think they know better.	» Perhaps they have an opinion that's worth hearing.
» These people don't take me seriously.	» What can I learn from their feedback?
» They're just out to make my life difficult.	» This must be a sensitive topic—I wonder what buttons I've pushed?
» They're more interested in looking good in front of the CEO than actually looking at the merit of my proposal.	» What do I need to do to make sure they feel included, that they've been heard?
» They're so self-absorbed, not willing to look past their own patch.	» It's up to me to help them see the merit in this idea, but ultimately they will be the ones who decide.

An abundance mindset

Just as the process of seeking other people's buy-in is likely to mean you will encounter people who are different from you, you are equally likely to encounter ideas, requests, disputes and demands that challenge your own. When you ask for x, someone else will want y. When you ask for additional budget allocation for your project, someone else will suggest their project deserves priority. When you ask your colleagues to focus on one set of tasks, someone will say they need to complete a different project first. You suggest a holiday in Paris; your spouse says we need to save for the bathroom renovation. Get my drift?

How do you respond in the face of this kind of pushback? How do you respond when someone says 'No' (or something less polite)? Do you begin to work out how best to assert and defend your own position? Or do you start asking yourself whether there might be a solution that will work for both of you?

This is your *abundance mindset* at play, and it sits in contrast to a scarcity mindset — both terms coined by Stephen R. Covey, author of *The 7 Habits of Highly Effective People*. An abundance mindset enters a conversation or negotiation with the starting assumption that there are plenty of fish in the proverbial sea. There's plenty to go around, if we're creative and clever about it.

A scarcity mindset, on the other hand, starts with the assumption that every gain to you comes at a cost to me; a dollar in your hand is a dollar lost for me. Perhaps this comes from an in-built survival instinct, knowing that there were only so many berries to pick as we crossed the great plains. Or maybe we've been well trained to believe we really must 'Hurry, while stocks last!'

AT ITS CORE, AN ABUNDANCE MINDSET REQUIRES US TO HAVE GREAT TRUST IN OUR ABILITY TO ACHIEVE A GOOD RESULT WITHOUT HAVING CONTROL OVER THE FINAL OUTCOME.

This is why leaders with an abundance mindset are far more comfortable allowing others to come up with new ideas, and letting people in their team take the reins on projects and initiatives. They understand that by allowing space for others to create — by yielding some of their control, as it were — the final outcome is likely to be a richer one.

WHAT ARE YOU SCARED OF?

Are any of the following reactions familiar to you?

» When someone criticises your proposal, your first instinct is to defend your own ideas and arguments, or strike back with a comment like, 'Well, have you got a *better* idea?'

» When someone flatly rejects your ideas, you dig your heels in ('Well, I'm afraid we really don't have any other options') or throw up your arms and abandon the conversation ('Fine, have it your way').

» When someone makes an alternative proposal, you state all the reasons you can't agree, in the hope that the discussion will get back to your original idea.

All of the above send a message to the other person: *It's your proposal against mine. Game on!* Which is likely to trigger the other person's scarcity mindset too. Watching a conversation between two scarcity mindsets can be like watching two tennis players fighting out a fiercely contested point. The tension is high and everyone is waiting for the moment when one player will get the upper hand.

To be successful at buy-in, you must work hard to foster and maintain an abundance mindset — not just in yourself, but in others too. When you adopt an abundant mindset, you go into every conversation with the view that there's a wide range of possible outcomes that could work for all parties, but that the only way to get there is through discussion, negotiation and debate.

JUST AS AN INCLUSIVE MINDSET LOOKS FOR DIFFERENCES, AN ABUNDANCE MINDSET ADOPTS THE VIEW THAT CONFLICT IS A GOOD THING. IT'S A PATH TO GROWTH.

Table 2.3 demonstrates the kinds of responses you can consciously adopt to change a scarcity mindset into an abundance one.

Table 2.3: a scarcity vs abundance response

Your scarcity response	Your abundance response
» My way is the best way.	» How can we craft a proposal that will account for all the different points of view in the room?
» I've worked hard on this proposal.	
» These people aren't giving me enough air-time to let me state my case.	» The more I let them debate and express their point of view on this, the more likely we are to get to a good outcome.
» They all think they've got a better idea, but they really don't have a clue.	
» Do they seriously think their idea could work?	» If I am clear about the rationale for this, and can account for their concerns, we can reach a better outcome.

Choosing what's possible?

Even for those of us who often choose inclusive over alien, and abundance over scarcity, biases and deep-seated assumptions will kick in from time to time, triggering an alien and scarcity response. That's just part of being human.

There's no magic pill that will help you to maintain a *what's possible?* stance; there's no free software to download. The key is to choose a *what's possible?* stance, and then to set about fostering one. Do you see the value of *what's possible?* Do you accept that seeing differences as alien and resources as scarce can hamper your endeavours to build the kind of genuine dialogue that will allow your target audience the space to buy in?

MAKE THE COMMITMENT NOW TO BE INCLUSIVE, ASSUME ABUNDANCE AND EXPLORE *WHAT'S POSSIBLE?*

In fact, write those two words down before you go into any conversation where your aim is to build agreement and buy-in: *'what's possible?'*

You might even adopt some of the statements listed in each of the columns headed 'An inclusive response' and 'An abundance response' in tables 2.2 and 2.3 as personal mantras. A mantra operates as a form of self-coaching: a seed you consciously and repeatedly sow in your mind as a way of short-circuiting your hardwired thinking. The key here is to keep coming back to the mantra — for example by repeating it, or by creating a highly visible reminder that will keep tapping you on the shoulder each day. That way, over time, the mantra comes to dominate your thinking (rather than your instinct).

Mindset is also the kind of thing that really benefits from another person's perspective. Make your choice to cultivate a *what's possible?* stance the focus of a conversation with a trusted colleague — perhaps even a coach. Discuss how the different underlying mindsets play out for you at different times, and where they are coming from. Challenge the rationality of these assumptions, and discuss ways you can keep the choice of inclusiveness and abundance present for yourself.

Over to you

Think of a situation you have been in where you faced pushback or resistance to an idea or proposal.

(Continued)

Over to you *(Cont'd)*

- » What aspects of the way you felt at the time indicate an alien mindset or an inclusive mindset?

- » What about a scarcity mindset or an abundance mindset?

- » Get together with a colleague, friend or coach, and talk through this exercise. Share examples of how the alien and scarcity mindsets play out for you. Do you tend to default to an alien or a scarcity mindset with certain people more than with others? Why?

- » Look back at the columns headed 'Your inclusive response' and 'Your abundance response' in tables 2.2 and 2.3. Jot down two or three statements or questions that you can use as a mantra to help you to make the shift to a *what's possible?* stance in the context of one of your own ideas or initiatives. Try repeating these questions to yourself before any kind of communication with your target audience on an idea or proposal — whether it's a meeting, a presentation or even an email — as a way of coaching yourself into a *what's possible?* stance.

* * *

As we've seen in this chapter, the quest for buy-in begins with a clear choice. Champions of buy-in choose 'win me' over 'decree', and then work hard to align the way they seek to influence others with that choice. We've explored how much easier this becomes when you take a *what's possible?* stance, which combines an inclusive mindset and a mindset of abundance. Now we're ready to begin exploring what it takes to build buy-in. And, as we're about to discover, it all starts with you.

CHAPTER 3
CONVICTION
Establish a 'Big So What'

'Believe you can and you're halfway there.'
Theodore Roosevelt

Scan your mind for those managers, colleagues, contractors and team members who seem to really care about their job. How does their passion and commitment impact on you? When they present a new idea to you, is their enthusiasm infectious? Are you willing to listen to them, to consider their ideas and be open to their influence more readily than others are? Do you find yourself yelling, 'Yes, yes!' when they ask you if you're in?

Truly influential people *believe* in their ideas. As one client, a senior manager in a digital company, once explained to me:

> If someone comes into my office asking for support on an idea, the first thing I assess is whether their heart is in it. Is their own battery pack plugged in and ready to go? If I don't see that, if I don't feel it, then I probably won't trust that person to get the job done. Have they done their homework? Are they thinking about this project on the train, in the shower, while they eat their lunch? Have they got the

passion to go out there and drum up support and—even more importantly—to weather the storm they will inevitably face? If there's a hint of doubt on those, then why would I give them the support they want?

You could read this book, participate in a training course, learn all the practical techniques needed to convince others of your ideas, but building buy-in is a bit like knowing how to dance the salsa. You can get up on the dance floor when the music kicks in, but if you're not enjoying yourself, if your heart isn't in the music, then it's only ever going to be a bunch of dance moves — and you'll probably have that terrified look on your face that makes everyone feel nervous and awkward.

So before we start looking at the things you can do to build buy-in from others, look into the mirror and ask yourself one crucial question: How convinced of your idea are *you*?

'Conviction up!'

In the people who come to my workshops, the one thing I can often sense is missing is their own conviction. You can hear it in their voice, sense it in their demeanour and see it in their eyes (that is, if they make eye contact at all). It's, well, underwhelming.

> TO GET OTHER PEOPLE TO BUY INTO YOUR IDEAS, *YOU* NEED TO BUY IN FIRST—OR, AS I LIKE TO CALL THIS, YOU NEED TO *CONVICTION UP!*

Conviction doesn't just mean being confident that your idea will work. The idea has to matter to you, just as you want it to matter to others. Your belief needs to be strong enough to fuel your perseverance in the face of resistance and doubt, and to push through those moments when things stall and seem to go backwards. After all, if you're not sold on your idea, why would I be?

There's a big difference between someone who throws their heart and soul into an idea and someone who is just going through the motions. I call these two very different people the *courier* and the *catalyst*. Let's look at each of them in turn.

THE COURIER

Couriers (as we know) deliver packages. So if we picture a courier as a type of influencer, then this means they are good at delivering information and letting people know about an idea or initiative — but that's the extent of their commitment. The courier doesn't have the conviction that's needed to take ownership of an idea and get others on board with it. If other people don't like the idea, the courier might declare, 'Hey, don't shoot the messenger!' Or they'll throw up their hands and say, 'I'm just doing what I was asked to do. If you don't like it, speak to the boss.'

Most of us would confess to playing the courier at work on occasion. It's very easy to get caught in this role when you're juggling multiple projects and struggling to get excited by some/any/all of them, especially if one of the projects has been handed to you by your manager with the instruction to 'just make it happen' (more on how to deal with that later in this chapter). What if an initiative you're working on feels necessary and unavoidable, but simply doesn't float your boat? In situations like this, you might find that being a courier is enough to get the job done, but if you really want to step up and have others chomping at the bit to help you launch a successful new project, then you must become a true champion of buy-in. That means moving from being a courier to being a *catalyst*.

THE CATALYST

Catalysts care. They want not only to initiate a change but to *achieve* that change. Catalysts see themselves as instrumental in that outcome. They don't stop at the point of resistance — quite the opposite. They put on their leadership leggings, roll up their sleeves, and ask themselves, 'What can I do to help this person?'

CATALYSTS DON'T REST UNTIL THEY SEE THE CHANGE BECOME A REALITY. CATALYSTS ARE TRUE INFLUENCERS.

Sometimes catalysts feel cursed by their appetite for change. 'I wish I could go home at 5 o'clock and stop caring,' they say when they feel vulnerable. Yet deep down, they know they wouldn't have it any other away, because the next morning they've got something to get up for and pursue with true conviction.

THE PASSION AND COMMITMENT OF A CATALYST IS INFECTIOUS: THEY CAN QUICKLY START A CHAIN REACTION, INSPIRING OTHERS TO BECOME CATALYSTS ALONG THE WAY.

This is why, even if you're not the one to be the catalyst on a project or initiative, it can be just as effective if you have others in your team who *do* have the requisite belief — provided those people are given the clearance to step up.

Be a catalyst

It's easy to assume that some people are just born catalysts. That these people wake up in the morning, slam down a can of go-get-'em juice, and spring into the workplace declaring at the top of their voice, 'Who's ready to be awesome today?' If you're not one of those people, it may seem as though the idea of being a catalyst is beyond your reach (or appetite). Perhaps you're telling yourself, 'I'll settle for courier, thanks.'

The good news is that being a catalyst is not about evangelical fervour, which can be a real turn-off for many people. Being a catalyst starts with a quietly held belief in the idea you're asking others to buy into.

CONVICTION DOESN'T ALWAYS JUST FALL FROM THE HEAVENS AND FILL YOUR SOUL. SOMETIMES YOU NEED TO *CHOOSE* TO GET CONVINCED.

You may often need to find the conviction in your idea, doing some hard work — yes, work — to build up your belief.

There is a process you can follow to build up your conviction in any idea:

1. Establish a *Big So What*.

2. Romance your purpose.

Let's work through these steps together now.

Establish a Big So What

Positive influence starts with absolute clarity about what it is exactly you're asking people to buy into, what it is you want to see change. People don't buy 'vibes'. They need to know exactly what it is you're asking of them. Without this, you'll struggle to get past first base.

But having a clear *what* isn't enough on its own. It might be enough for the courier, but catalysts need more to drive a change. They need to know *why* it matters — to you, to them, to anyone else. All the other stuff is just technical detail and logistics.

There is a fantastic TED talk by Simon Sinek called 'How great leaders inspire action'. If you aren't familiar with it then I highly recommend you stop reading and watch it now. Sinek sums it up perfectly when he says, 'People don't buy what you do, they buy why you do it.'

My favourite method for getting a really strong *why* is to identify a *Big So What*. Your *Big So What* poses and then answers the question: Why does this idea matter? I mean, *really*. (Think of a less-than-convinced teenager sitting opposite you, arms crossed and with a disbelieving look on their face. 'So what?')

The process of discovering the *Big So What* will help you to refine your idea until you get to something others will think is worth buying into.

Let's look at a practical example of how this works.

Melissa is working on a project that centralises all of the customer information kept by the company in a single database. In the past, different company divisions — each of which deals with customers at different stages of the customer relationship — has developed its own unique way of storing customer data. As a result, it's near impossible to get a complete customer history without going to each department and asking them to share their own information. This is a time-consuming and sensitive process, with teams fiercely protective of their customer records. To be successful, Melissa is going to need to get buy-in from thirty executives and she's anticipating plenty of pushback. Feeling a little anxious, Melissa sits down to try to define the project:

Project: Bring customer data into a single place.
Why? Make it easier for people to get a whole view of the customer – something we've been struggling with for a while.
So what? Otherwise we miss opportunities.
So what? Our competitors will seize them.
So what? Lose customers, market position drops, revenue drops, morale drops.

> **Big So What:** This project is about protecting our market position as a premium supplier in the market. Without being able to look our customers in the eye and say we have a whole view of them, we shouldn't be surprised when our competitors come in and snatch customers from under our nose.

Notice how each time Melissa asks herself 'So what' she gets closer to the bigger picture, until she finally feels she's nailed the *Big So What*. This idea started out as just another action on her to-do list, with a fairly basic rationale, but now it's a key strategic activity for the company — something she's sure her senior managers and colleagues throughout the company will be convinced of.

Romance your purpose

Now you've identified your idea's *Big So What*, it's time to become intimate with it. Remember, as the days and weeks go by, you're going to get caught up doing other stuff and it's going to be easy to lose sight of why you initiated the idea in the first place.

Relationships are the same. A relationship can exist between two people, but when you both get busy and forget to take time out to reconnect — talk, go to dinner, see a movie, take a weekend away together — it's very easy to feel like you're going in separate directions.

This is why you've got to make an effort to *romance your purpose*. This means regularly sitting with, and reflecting and meditating on, why you're doing this project — in other words, your *Big So What*.

A few years ago, I went on a yoga retreat in the country. Our instructor on the retreat, Amy, said something that really struck a chord with me. She urged us to think of yoga not just as a bunch of moves or as a process. Instead she said we should reflect on our purpose for doing yoga, and stay focused on that throughout our practice. This is a powerful lesson for those of us who are seeking buy-in.

TO ENGAGE OTHERS, YOU MUST HAVE A CLEAR PURPOSE AND STRONG CONVICTION AT ALL TIMES. THE BUSIER YOU GET, THE HARDER THIS BECOMES. SO IT IS IMPERATIVE THAT YOU KEEP COMING BACK REGULARLY TO THE SOURCE OF ENERGY, PURPOSE AND YOUR *WHY*.

Spend time with your idea. Persuade yourself why it's a good one, in much the same way you will have to persuade others. Develop a clear argument for your idea and keep refining that argument. Sit down with colleagues or a coach or mentor to work through any ifs and buts that may arise.

Work through difficulties and allow time for lightbulb moments of clarity. I know mine usually come when I go for a long walk or when I talk the idea through out loud to myself. This is a way of processing that helps to shush the internal critic that often fills our head with unhelpful self-talk like, *You've got no idea what you're saying. They can see right through you. Abort, abort!*

THE MORE TIME YOU ALLOW TO WORK THROUGH AN IDEA AT VARIOUS STAGES OF IMPLEMENTATION, THE BETTER YOUR CHANCE OF TURNING YOUR INTERNAL CRITIC INTO YOUR INTERNAL CHEER SQUAD.

Let's face it, there will be times when you're responsible for implementing an idea or initiative that just doesn't get you pumped, or worse, you've been told you 'just have to do it'. Here are some helpful strategies for overcoming these types of problem children.

'BUT THE BOSS SAID ...'

What if your manager has asked you to take on a project, idea or initiative, and to 'just make it happen'? Suddenly you're left holding the proverbial baby, and faced with the daunting task of getting others to help you raise it. Before you know it, you're standing in front of your team, showing them the baby and saying, 'Work with me, people!' They're all looking back at you saying, 'Why?' And your only response is, 'Because the boss said we have to!' This leaves you playing the uninspiring role of courier. It's going to be a long, hard slog to get buy-in from here.

So what do you do?

Imagine you freeze-framed the moment your manager delegated the project to you and you politely but firmly asked them to take the time to help you to understand why this idea or project is a good one. What if you said, 'If you want me to get people to buy into this, then I need to know the *Big So What*'?

When I make this point in my workshops, I see people squirm in their seat, uncomfortable with the prospect of being so impertinent with their boss, or perhaps with the prospect of having to deal with their manager's reaction. But consider this: your manager may not have been able to get that clarity from *their* manager before it was delegated to them. In which case, the process needs you to create some upwards pressure to tackle that gap. Also, look at it this way: your manager may have so much going on that they simply haven't made it a priority to help you, so unless you ask, you won't get!

DUD DATES

Ever been in a relationship with someone far longer than you wanted to be? Or on a date that didn't feel like it was going anywhere?

If you're landed with an initiative that you're really struggling with, and you just can't find a way to get your own conviction up, then there are two questions to ask yourself:

1. Am I the right person to lead this idea? Or is someone else better placed to build buy-in because of their utter conviction about the project?

2. Is it enough for me to play the courier here? Is this the right situation for me to just stand and deliver?

These aren't always easy questions to answer on your own. It might help to ask a mentor or trusted colleague to help assess where you stand so you can choose your next steps. It's a case of not giving up too soon just because it's hard, but also knowing when to draw a line in the sand and walk away.

Top tip

Even a champion like Muhammad Ali had to work very hard on fostering conviction. It's not something he simply woke up with every day. As he once said, 'It's the repetition of affirmations that leads to belief. And once that belief becomes a deep conviction, things begin to happen.'

Over to you

1. Think of an idea or initiative you're currently working on. Are you playing the role of courier or catalyst?

2. Develop a *Big So What* for the same idea or initiative. Work through the following steps using the example provided in this chapter as a guide:
    »   What's the idea or proposal?
    »   Why does it matter?
    »   Ask yourself, 'So what?'
    »   Keep asking, 'So what?' until you come to the heart of the matter.
    »   What's the *Big So What*?

* * *

Is your conviction up? Are you fuelled by a clear *Big So What*? Are you ready to step into the role of catalyst? If you're feeling pumped and ready to start rallying others around your idea, then you need to consider: *Who* do you rally? And in what order? Let's explore these questions in the next chapter.

CHAPTER 4
WHO
Think wide, act narrow

'If you want to go fast, go alone. To go far, go together.'
Old African proverb

In Leo Tolstoy's classic novel *Anna Karenina*, the young debutante princess Kitty focuses her devotions on Count Vronsky, a handsome army officer. When Vronsky turns his affections to Anna, Kitty descends into a pit of misery — until she comes to see that the path to her true happiness has been right under her nose all the time, in the form of her childhood friend Kostya Levin, whom Kitty has spurned. Kitty goes on to enjoy a wonderful life with Levin, while Vronsky becomes Anna's tragic undoing.

Sure, this is fiction, and the story an extravagantly romantic one, but the plot echoes the familiar reality of waking up one day to realise that you have wasted your time and energy on the wrong person. Not a mistake you want to make when it comes to building buy-in and getting your ideas or initiatives off the ground.

Several years ago I was working with a group of sales managers in an agricultural business, most of whose customers were farmers. They were trying to work out a way of increasing the range of products purchased by some of their customers. I asked the group to explain how they typically approached a sales conversation with the farmers. The consensus was that most conversations were pretty spontaneous and informal, typically across a paddock fence. The group explained that this was the best way they had found to get time to talk to the customer and to build rapport.

At that moment, one of the newer members of the team interrupted: 'I grew up on a farm. My dad's a farmer, but I'll tell you something, if you tried to get him to buy new equipment without my mum being in the conversation, you wouldn't stand a chance.'

Some of the group looked quizzically back at the young sales person. She went on to explain that, in her house, it was her mother who controlled the budget and who played a key part in any decisions to invest in new equipment. It was a revelation for many in the room. They immediately realised they'd been leaving a key person out of their conversations.

Navigate the social landscape

Knowing who's who in the proverbial zoo is an essential part of getting heard and making your ideas a reality. Ask yourself these questions:

» Who's involved in making the ultimate decision about whether your idea goes ahead and how it is implemented?

» Who plays a key role in bringing your idea to life?

» Who could stand in the way?

» Who influences whom?

» Who might be able to help get others on board?

» Whose input is needed to ensure the final decision is a good one?

» Who expects to be consulted before a decision is made?

» What social norms and conventions do people expect you to follow?

» Who's *really* running the show?

Organisations are complex beasts. While the traditional organisational chart might be aimed at simplifying things by showing who reports to whom, the real picture of how things get done lies in the informal and often messy web of relationships that develops slowly over time. I call this the *social landscape*.

IF YOU DON'T UNDERSTAND THE SOCIAL LANDSCAPE BEFORE YOU BEGIN THE PROCESS OF BUY-IN, YOU'RE LIKELY TO COME UP AGAINST MYSTIFYING OBSTACLES AND RESISTANCE FROM DIRECTIONS YOU WERE LEAST EXPECTING.

'Organisational politics' — a term often used in a pejorative way to describe the intricate dynamics that make change hard — is very real in organisations.

THINK WIDE, ACT NARROW

In order to avoid being undermined by the complex social landscape, it's important to take the time to *choose your who's* — in other words, to make some well-informed decisions about whom you need to engage with to get your idea off the ground and into action successfully.

Top tip

At every step along the way, the champion of buy-in thinks wide while acting narrow. That is, they

(Continued)

45

> **Top tip** (*Cont'd*)
>
> have a wide-angled lens trained on the broader social landscape, even while engaged in an isolated, one-on-one conversation.

NEMAWASHI

Japanese culture embodies this idea in the form of a strong social norm called *nemawashi*, which literally means to prepare the roots of a tree before transplanting it. In the same way, nemawashi refers to the informal and gentle practice of taking the time to prepare the groundwork for an initiative by talking to the relevant people, gathering their input, feedback and support.

Nemawashi is important in Japanese culture at a number of levels. First, it demonstrates respect and reverence towards others by giving people an opportunity to express their opinion about an idea — most importantly, in a private conversation — before it is formally presented. Second, it allows people to feel confident that the right views have been sought out, making it more likely that the decision is a good one and will ultimately prosper.

Nemawashi may have little currency outside of Japan, but there is much to be learned from it. To the outsider, nemawashi can seem like a slow and painful process — all that talking, consulting, pre-meeting meetings ... *I mean, haven't we got work to do?* Therein lies the crucial lesson. An inclusive and consultative process requires time and patience, both often in short supply given the pace at which many organisations are used to operating.

While inclusive consultation may take time, the pay-off is actually rapid execution and action. This has been observed by Dunigan O'Keeffe, from global consulting firm Bain & Company, who has worked with Japanese organisations for many years: '[T]here's nothing fast about making bad decisions or suffering through a faulty implementation. Paradoxically, slowing down on the front end to gather the insights of those closest to the customer can end up creating the most speed when it counts.'[6]

Without clear focus and direction, the principle of nemawashi could lead you down a tunnel of endless conversations and consultations that make generating action a herculean task. So how do you focus your energy on the right person, at the right time, for the right reasons, in the right way?

Create a social map

If you're going to navigate the social landscape successfully, then it's a great idea to create a *social map*.

Social mapping is a simple technique you can use to zero in on the people who matter most to getting your idea or project off the ground. These are your *stakeholders*, a term that describes anyone who is likely to impact or be impacted by a decision.

Unlike the traditional organisational chart, a social map doesn't show reporting lines and hierarchy, which as we've already discussed may not give you much insight into who the real stakeholders are. Nor is a social map a generic map of relationships across the organisation. Rather, it's a map that you create in the context of thinking about a specific idea or proposal for which you're looking to generate buy-in.

Social mapping allows you to:

» **identify** all of the people relevant to turning your idea into a reality

» **assess** each person's role, their attitude towards your idea and how they fit into the social landscape

» **design** an ideal *sequence of engagement* — who you talk to first, second and so on.

CREATING A SOCIAL MAP IS LIKE DRAWING A MAP OF A SUBURB FOR THE FIRST TIME. YOU CAN ONLY DRAW WHAT YOU SEE, SO YOU HAVE TO BUILD IT SLOWLY, BIT BY BIT, AND KEEP MAKING ADJUSTMENTS OVER TIME.

There are five steps to creating a social map:

1. Identify your stakeholders.

2. Chart the influence.

3. Spot your allies

4. Review your map.

5. Create a sequence of engagement.

STEP 1: IDENTIFY YOUR STAKEHOLDERS

Who are the people who matter most for the purposes of getting your idea or initiative off the ground? Consider the following four categories of stakeholders:

1. **Decision maker.** This is the person who makes the ultimate decision that determines whether or not your idea actually gets off the ground. It's rare that there would be more than one person in this category. Unless the decision is being made by some kind of committee or panel, coming up with multiple people and names here suggests there's some confusion about who actually makes the crucial decisions.

2. **Influencers.** These are the people whose views may — or should — influence the decision maker,

directly or indirectly. This has nothing to do with rank and could even include people outside the organisation, such as technical experts and advisers.

3. **Implementers.** These people are instrumental in determining how an idea or project will be implemented. That might be the managers of teams responsible for bringing an idea to life, or it could be a whole group of operational people whose cooperation will be vital to the success of the initiative — people such as technical designers, account managers, engineers and frontline staff.

4. **Wildcards.** This last category refers to all those stakeholders who might *expect* a role, or expect to be informed or involved in some way, even though they don't have any formal involvement. Think of it like a mystery box that could spring open at any time (which is why you're trying to anticipate them now, before they surprise you). If you haven't already identified them in the other categories, consider stakeholders such as senior executives, employee unions, the in-house legal team, key customers or suppliers who may be affected by the project, and so on.

Every social map starts with a clear understanding of who sits in each of these categories. Of course, there's a real risk that you don't capture what you don't know. For example, do you have enough awareness of the social landscape to be able to identify all the Wildcards accurately? Given the aim here is to create as reliable a picture of the social landscape as possible, it can be useful to ask a trusted colleague for their perspective on the relevant stakeholders, as this may offer extra richness to your map.

STEP 2: CHART THE INFLUENCE

With your stakeholders clearly identified, it's time to grab a whiteboard or big sheet of paper and get your art into gear. Lots of white space is the key.

Using different colours for each the different categories of stakeholder (red for the decision maker, blue for influencers, and so on), map out all of the relevant stakeholders, drawing little circles for each person and writing their name or initials inside the circle.

This is where you need to resist the temptation to draw an organisational chart. Instead, you're charting the relationships of influence between the various stakeholders. That mightn't have anything to do with formal rank or reporting lines. Who listens to whom? Who turns to whom for advice or guidance? And, just as importantly, are there any stakeholder relationships that are broken to the point that there's a negative influence between them?

Once you start charting the relationships of influence, the complexity of the social landscape really comes to life. I like to use lines and arrows to denote the flow of influence between stakeholders — double-headed arrows if the influence flows in both directions, and heavier lines for stronger influence. Where there are dysfunctional relationships, I use a broken line.

Understanding these relationships is incredibly important for gauging how people really form views and make decisions. By assessing the social landscape in this way, you can start to work out whether you need to include certain stakeholders early on, either to harness the power of their influence, or to manage their potential to interfere with your own efforts to build buy-in (more on that in step 5).

STEP 3: SPOT YOUR ALLIES

Once you've charted the influence, you need to identify your potential allies. Allies are the people who are prepared to back you and to lend a hand. They're the ones who might introduce you to the right people and help to establish trust, or they might coach you through the social landscape by sharing their knowledge and understanding.

So how do you spot these allies? An ally may sit within the map you've created so far, or may even sit outside the scope of the four categories you worked through in step 1. According to Paul Weinstein, a sales expert and regular contributor to *Harvard Business Review*, allies 'rarely have significant power in the organization — but they know who does and their expertise is usually respected. [They] understand the personalities and processes on a granular level and can navigate the culture within an organization.'[7]

If nothing else, allies are great to have on hand as a kind of 'cheer squad'. These are the folks you can turn to for moral support and perhaps even a shoulder to cry on when you're feeling like you're facing some tough resistance. Who better to help reset your conviction and get you back into your catalyst state when the pushback you're experiencing takes its toll? (For all of these reasons, allies make great coffee dates.) Mark the allies on your map with a big star — no other symbol seems appropriate!

STEP 4: REVIEW YOUR MAP

Your social map is now probably looking something like the one in figure 4.1 (see overleaf).

Messy? Don't worry. Social maps aren't intended to be an instant picture of clarity. The first maps drawn by cartographers bore little resemblance to how we see things today, but at the time they were regarded as statements of 'truth'.

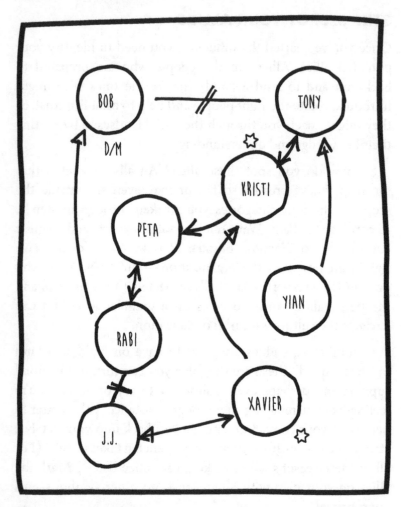

Figure 4.1: a social map

For this reason, it's important to revisit your map regularly, especially as you start interacting with different people and learn more about the lay of the land. And, if you've created the map all on your lonesome so far, now is the time to 'phone a friend', to mitigate the risk of your map being riddled with flawed assumptions.

WHAT YOUR SOCIAL MAP *DOES* REPRESENT IS YOUR ATTEMPT TO BETTER UNDERSTAND THE UNIQUE SOCIAL LANDSCAPE WITHIN WHICH YOU'RE WORKING, AND THE WAY RELATIONSHIPS ARE LIKELY TO HELP OR HINDER YOU IN GETTING THINGS DONE.

STEP 5: CREATE A SEQUENCE OF ENGAGEMENT

You're now in a position to *choose your who's* — to start making some informed choices about who to include in your *target audience*[8] and how you will engage with them. Who will you approach first? What do you hope to achieve at each step of the way? How will you approach each stakeholder (for example, informally over a coffee, by email or as part of a group workshop)? What are you anticipating each step might then lead to?

The best way to answer these questions is to create a *sequence of engagement*, such as the one in table 4.1 (see overleaf). Piecing together a sequence of engagement is a little like making a decision about the order in which to prepare the different elements of a three-course meal when you're hosting a dinner party. There's no one 'right' way to go about it, but certain sequences will help you to get to your desired outcome more than others. (If you leave churning the homemade ice cream until last, you may find yourself serving it as a runny *crème anglaise* instead.)

As wonderful as it would be to map out the entire sequence of engagement now, it's unlikely that you'll be able to predict much further than the first three steps, as the outcome of each is bound to shape what follows.

Table 4.1: sample sequence of engagement

Who?	Why?	How?
Paula (marketing team member)	Seek her advice on how best to approach Geoff R. (GM Marketing)	Informal chat (lunch?)
Geoff R. (GM Marketing)	Seek out his support to canvas the idea with the broader team	Catch-up (depends on Paula's advice)
Faizan (product team member)	Scope out the marketing team workshop and see if he's willing to facilitate it	Meeting

BE PURPOSEFUL

As you create your sequence of engagement, look for opportunities to do each of the following:

» **Enlist your allies.** How can you enlist the support of any allies early on? Seek their advice and guidance early. Ask them to review your social map and to coach you on the subtleties of the social landscape. Take the time to understand the role they can play in introducing you to important stakeholders.

» **Seek feedback.** Whose input or feedback is going to be helpful in developing your idea so it is in good shape to solicit people's support? This is a great chance not just to engage with those who may be raving fans, but also to speak early on with the potential naysayers or critics of your idea. What can you learn from them that will help you to refine your idea and to overcome potential objections?

» **Create connections.** Who do you need to involve early for the purposes of getting them onside and building trust? In the same way that the Japanese principle of nemawashi expects consultation as a social norm, so too do many organisations and teams. Include these folk early so as not to get key stakeholders offside.

» **Build a bandwagon.** Who is likely to be an early supporter of your idea? Getting those people on board early on may help you reach an all-important 'tipping point' (defined by Malcolm Gladwell as 'the moment of critical mass, the threshold, the boiling point'[9]) for getting momentum on your idea. That momentum can also have a gravitational pull on the other stakeholders through what behavioural economist Daniel Kahneman refers to as the 'bandwagon effect', causing others to hop on board too.

» **Nurture the naysayers.** Sun Tzu once wrote, 'Keep your friends close and your enemies closer' (advice echoed by Don Corleone in *The Godfather*). While it can be tempting to steer a wide berth around them or put them in the 'too hard' basket, naysayers may be intrinsic to getting your idea off the ground. There's a risk that naysayers may only become more entrenched in their position if they feel neglected. Naysayers may also be influential, so keeping close to them enables you to monitor the impact they may have on others while you gently try to turn them into supporters.

» **Close the loop.** Consider who else needs to be kept informed. In the case of larger groups, that might be by communicating regular updates or information through an agreed channel (such as an online discussion board, emails or regular 'town hall' style forums). If there are only a few people in this category, you might opt for a more personalised form of communication — regular conversations, emails or perhaps even handwritten notes. The aim here is to make this low effort to you, but high value to your stakeholders.

A SHIFTING LANDSCAPE

Social map in hand, the time has come to get ready to take those first steps towards engaging with your target audience — the stakeholders you've included in your sequence of engagement.

IT'S IMPORTANT TO REMEMBER THAT BOTH YOUR SOCIAL MAP AND SEQUENCE OF ENGAGEMENT ARE LIKELY TO BE MOVING FEASTS. WITH THIS IN MIND, CONTINUALLY REVISIT BOTH OF THESE, MAKING ADJUSTMENTS AS YOU LEARN MORE ABOUT THE SOCIAL LANDSCAPE AND THE DIFFERENT STAKEHOLDERS' PERSPECTIVES.

Be attuned too to sudden changes in the social landscape. Relationships of influence and organisational dynamics take years to form. But, just as an earthquake can suddenly rip apart a terrain that is thousands of years old, the social landscape too can be disrupted in an instant. Sudden changes of staff, shifts in role, relationship breakdowns — all of these things can turn the way decisions get made on its head.

Over to you

Create your own social map for an idea or initiative you're working on or have worked on in the past. Using a large sheet of paper or a whiteboard, work through each of the social mapping steps in this chapter:

1. **Identify your stakeholders.** Map out the various stakeholders, using the four categories *Decision-maker, Influencer, Implementers* and *Wildcards*. Avoid clumping stakeholders together (try to draw circles for every stakeholder on the map), and make sure you don't draw an organisational chart. Include yourself in the map, too.

2. **Chart the influence.** Map out the relationships of influence between the stakeholders using lines and arrows. Also identify any broken relationships where the influence might be negative.

3. **Spot your allies.** Who on your map might be an ally? Also consider whether there are others not currently on the map who could play this important role.

4. **Review your map (step 4) and create a sequence of engagement (step 5).** Stand back and start mapping out the initial stages of the ideal sequence of engagement. Identify who to engage at each step, for what purpose (*why*) and the general nature of your approach (*how*). Who will you approach first and why?

* * *

In this chapter, we've assessed the complex web of relationships that make or break the way things get done in the typical organisation. Once you *choose your who's* (or as Dr Seuss might have said, once you've 'choosen your who-sen'), it's time to begin thinking about how you can best engage with your target audience to ensure you have the best chance of gaining their buy-in. That starts with a sound understanding of the wider picture. Let me explain in chapter 5.

CHAPTER 5
TIMING
Read the conditions, ride the wave

'Adapt or perish, now as ever, is nature's inexorable imperative.'
H. G. Wells

For many people living on the coast in Australia, surfing is a part of everyday outdoor life. So when I went for my first surf at age 41 I felt like I was embarking on a sort of belated rite of passage (and my kids were most impressed).

My surf coach, Cliff, looked like your classic Aussie surfer: shaggy blond hair, rusted-on tan and lips caked in zinc sunscreen. We stood at the top of the stairs leading down to the beach, both looking out at the ocean. Cliff turned to me and said, 'First thing you need to do before going anywhere near the water is assess the conditions.' He pointed to the waves, asking me if they were spilling, crashing, surging or dumping (ah ... I had no idea). Where was the rip — the strong and often dangerous crosscurrent? He dissected the conditions for me, blow by blow, and announced, 'The surf today is good! Some days I'd tell you to get in your car and come back another time.'

Even when we finally got out to the spot where the waves were breaking, we sat on our boards for what seemed like forever, waiting for the right wave (or for a shark to bite off my leg). Surfing, I learned, requires a lot of patience and a willingness to adapt to the conditions. If the waves are wild and messy, you'll find it really difficult to surf. If the waves are too big or breaking way offshore, you exert all your energy just paddling out. According to Cliff, you need to take all of these factors into account.

The same principle applies when it comes to seeking people's buy-in to your ideas and initiatives. As you engage with people, no matter how much they might love your idea in theory, in reality their energy, attention and attitude are all likely to be affected by other forces. You are competing with these forces, which I call the *prevailing conditions*.

Conditions for buy-in

As you read this chapter, how do the prevailing conditions around you affect your ability to absorb and engage with the content? Are you focused or distracted? Is there too much noise to concentrate? Have you got enough time to sit and reflect on the ideas presented here and how they might apply to you? What's going on in your world right now that might distract you or make it harder to apply the ideas you come across in this book?

While it might be hard — almost impossible — to account for all of these conditions during the process of actually writing a book, you can try to anticipate and account for factors that might be affecting your target audience's ability to engage with you and your idea.

For example, when I'm running a workshop, I spend time a few days in advance of the workshop date speaking with my clients, trying to understand what's currently affecting them, what's happening in their business, and how this is likely to impact on the workshop participants. I try my best to account for these conditions when I design and facilitate the actual sessions. Sometimes I'll even consider whether it might be best to reschedule the workshop entirely to a more favourable time — one that will ensure my client gets the most value from the workshop.

So what are the prevailing conditions we need to be on the lookout for?

» **Mood.** The organisation's results have just been announced, and they're disappointing. The CEO has issued an all-staff memo flagging the likelihood that budget cuts will be needed — or worse, redundancies are on the horizon. Morale has taken a dive. Everyone's feeling it, including the group of people you were planning to pitch a new idea to. How does this sudden downturn in mood affect the way you approach your project pitch? Setting the right mood for buy-in and understanding all the sensitivities involved is a critical step, which is why I've dedicated a lot more space to it in chapter 7.

> **TRYING TO BUILD BUY-IN WITHOUT UNDERSTANDING THE PREVAILING MOOD OF YOUR AUDIENCE IS LIKE WALKING INTO A FUNERAL WHISTLING 'I'M WALKING ON SUNSHINE'.**

» **Distractions.** Are there loud building works next to your meeting room? Is a fire alarm going off? Or has the team just been told that Sally is engaged and everyone's busy asking questions and squealing with delight? These are all distractions that may require you to wait until the

excitement subsides or even to relocate or reschedule
the conversation. But then there are things that may not
be quite so *audibly* loud but are equally distracting, such
as conflicting priorities, urgent phone calls, sudden staff
changes, a customer complaint or the IT system going
down. Persevering in the face of these kinds of
distractions is often a futile exercise.

» **Priorities.** What other projects or ideas have people got
on their plates right now? What demands do they have
on their attention and energy? It's important to be
sensitive to this and consider whether now is the right
time to approach a particular person and/or group. If
your target audience is in a mad dash to meet a project
deadline, trying to get their attention on other matters
might be a wasted opportunity. Or if they are about to
go on a two-week holiday to Fiji, you may find the only
new ideas they're willing to hear are ones that will help
them get out the door faster.

» **People.** Understanding the social landscape, who you're
targeting and the way in which your audience operates is
a crucial skill, which is why we explored it in detail in
chapter 4. This intricate web of relationships has the
power to derail your idea before it even gets out of the
station. Failing to take it into account at the start of your
project can slow you down or even bring your entire
initiative to a screeching halt. Map that social landscape!

Read the play

In the sporting world, there's a concept called 'reading the
play'. This refers to the way some players read the game as it's
unfolding and make judgements about how to adapt to the
game.

PLAYERS WHO ARE GOOD AT READING THE PLAY ARE ABLE TO MAKE INTUITIVE DECISIONS ABOUT WHEN TO ADOPT AN OFFENSIVE RATHER THAN A DEFENSIVE STRATEGY, WHEN TO HAND-OFF TO ANOTHER MEMBER OF THE TEAM, WHEN TO SLOW THE GAME DOWN OR SPEED IT UP, AND WHEN TO HOLD BACK.

In much the same way, champions of buy-in are good at reading the play and adjusting their strategies. They know that if they fail to adapt and adjust to prevailing conditions, then their message or idea could be undermined — or worse, it could fall on deaf ears.

'IT'S LIKE HERDING CATS'

A few years back, I had the opportunity to pitch to run a program for a group of leaders in a professional services firm. I was invited to come in and present my proposal to a panel comprising some of the leaders for whom the program was intended. I arrived at reception and was greeted by a woman with an exasperated look on her face. 'Is everything okay?' I asked her. 'Yes,' she replied, 'although I've had to do some last-minute running around to make sure we've got an audience for you. Everyone I *thought* was coming pulled out at the last minute. It's been like herding cats.'

My heart sank. Why would these leaders be pulling out? So I asked her, 'Is that a sign of anything? I assumed they were all keen to be involved.' She replied, 'Well, they *were* keen to veto whoever we choose, but they seem less interested in getting the program off the ground in the first place.'

Feeling my confidence shaken, I quickly thought through what to do. It was clear that the conditions weren't what I'd been expecting. The group's focus was elsewhere, they were distracted and the mood was, at best, cynical. To top it off, a few minutes later I found myself in a cramped room with a dodgy data projector that was clearly not about to play ball either.

63

One thing was immediately clear to me: everything had to change. I'd come to make a presentation and I no longer had anything to present with. I'd come to position myself as the ideal facilitator for their program, but that wasn't something they were interested in. I sat down in front of the group, closed my laptop, exhaled, and said, 'So ... I've been given a brief and I've put together a proposal, which I'm happy to present to you, but what I really want to know is: who are *you* and what do *you* want?' I sat silently for a few, very long moments, until one of the group declared, 'That's a *good question.*' And then, turning to his colleagues: 'What *do* we want?' And so began an hour of open discussion about their real objectives. Consequently, I got the gig.

This example shows what it means to read the play. In a very short space of time, I had to:

» assess the prevailing conditions

» listen to my instinct that the approach I had planned needed to change

» trust myself to let go of my script and find a meaningful way to connect with my audience

» get comfortable with some silence and puzzled looks as I took the conversation in an unexpected direction.

A situation like this can be like downing a triple-shot espresso — suddenly you feel your heart beating faster and your palms are sweaty. *Do I or don't I change the plan?* But what's the alternative?

IF YOU PLOUGH STRAIGHT INTO THE PREVAILING CONDITIONS KNOWING FULL WELL THAT THE BRAKES ARE ON, THE WARNING LIGHTS ARE FLASHING AND EVERYONE'S YELLING, *'RUN FOR YOUR LIVES!'*, THEN YOU'RE ASKING FOR A WIPEOUT.

What situation would you rather be in?

TIMING IS EVERYTHING

There's a funny routine performed by comedian Rowan Atkinson that goes:

A: I say, I say, I say, what is the secret to good comedy?
B: I don't know, what is the secret to g—
A. (While B is still talking) Timing.
B: What?
A: Timing!

If timing is the secret to good comedy, the same should be said for generating buy-in. A crucial aspect of reading the play is knowing when to pitch your idea — and knowing when to put it on hold.

A client of mine, Tim,[10] is an executive who learned this the hard way. He'd spent months preparing a business case to present to his boss, proposing a new marketing strategy that would attract a new type of customer to the business. Tim scheduled a meeting with the company's regional Managing Director to present his business case. He was excited not just about the potential of the proposal, but also about the opportunity to demonstrate his initiative to the MD. As it happened, a few days before Tim's meeting, the MD made a company-wide announcement of worse-than-expected financial performance. The MD said the company had spent too much time and energy on new, unproven strategies and declared they would now need to come back to their core business — the stuff they know works.

In spite of this news, Tim went ahead and presented his strategy at the MD's leadership meeting that week. As he outlined the key elements of his proposal, the MD grimaced, 'Sorry to interrupt, Tim, but I'm trying to see how this is going to fit with the announcement I made on Monday. You did hear that announcement, didn't you?' Tim *had* heard the announcement, but he'd invested so much time into preparing for this meeting, and invested so much of *himself* in the opportunity to present it to the leadership team, that he'd fallen into the all-too-easy trap of becoming myopically focused on his own objectives. As a result, Tim wasted the potential in his proposal by presenting it at completely the wrong time, and probably emerged from that meeting with a dent in his credibility as a leader.

Top tip

Catholic Archbishop Fulton Sheen once said, 'Patience is power. Patience is not an absence of action; rather it is timing. It waits on the right time to act, for the right principles and in the right way.' Champions of buy-in understand this. They have a well-honed ability to adjust their approach wherever possible so that they are working *with* the conditions, not against them. This book may be titled *Get Heard, Get Results*, but neither of those things are going to happen unless you adapt to your context. At times, as with surfing, this may mean you need to turn around, go back to the car and wait until conditions are more favourable.

A senior manager I know had been planning an offsite meeting for his management team, with the objective of allowing the team to review its focus for the next six months and, perhaps more significantly, its own dynamics as a team. The offsite had been planned for some months, accommodation booked and flights paid, but two weeks before kick-off date, the leader made the bold decision to postpone it. Why?

A few days earlier, the CEO had indicated his intention to review the company's structure, citing confusing reporting lines and slow progress on key change initiatives as the major reasons. Although there was no concrete information about when that review would happen, or how it would affect the team in question, the manager recognised how hard it would be for the team to focus on the questions he wanted to address at the offsite, because of the new uncertainty caused by the CEO's announcement.

On the one hand, the timing seemed unfortunate. On the other, it was a blessing. Had the CEO's announcement come *after* the offsite, the ensuing restructure might have rendered the whole thing a waste of time.

Ride the waves

It's true that you can't always control or completely avoid the prevailing conditions. Teams often tell me that they live in a perpetual maelstrom of adverse conditions: rapidly changing priorities, mixed messages from senior leadership, a revolving door in the management suite, and so on. As much as they may try, there's a limit to what they can do to mitigate these rolling effects.

So how do you learn to adjust and adapt to that kind of uncertainty? The best advice I've heard is to 'keep it simple — one idea at a time, one day at a time — and persist'. Persistence is like trying to crack a Sudoku puzzle. It might take a few rounds of trial and error, but once you've got a couple of numbers then all the rest start to fall into place. What a great feeling!

REMEMBER, FOR ALL THE TIMES THE PREVAILING CONDITIONS WORK AGAINST YOU, THERE WILL BE AN EQUAL – IF NOT GREATER – NUMBER OF TIMES WHEN THEY WORK IN YOUR FAVOUR.

Exactly the same can be said about waiting for the perfect wave to surf.

Over to you

Think of an idea or initiative you are currently working on that you are trying to get people to buy into.

1. What prevailing conditions are you working against — mood, distractions, priorities and/or people? How are they affecting your ability to engage your target audience, and with what result?

2. How well have you read the play? How could you adjust your approach so you are working *with* those conditions not against them?

* * *

In this chapter, we looked at the broader environment within which you're seeking to get heard and create buy-in. We examined the way prevailing conditions can impact our ability even to capture the attention of our target audience, let alone to secure their cooperation. By reading the play, champions of buy-in look for ways to adjust their approach to account for those conditions. Now, there's one final ingredient to get ready for success — and it starts with the question: Why would anyone listen to *you*?

CHAPTER 6
YOU
Be someone they'll listen to

'Character may almost be called the most effective means
of persuasion.'
Aristotle

I was sitting in a café with my client Susan while we did some planning together for an upcoming conference. Susan's phone rang. 'Sorry,' she said, glancing at the screen. She identified the caller, rolled her eyes and turned the phone face down on the table. 'No thank you,' she said with a sigh, as if she was speaking to the rejected caller.

'Bad news?' I asked.

'He's hard work — and he only started with our business a few months ago.'

How do you think this person (whoever the caller was) was going to achieve anything in the company if he couldn't get others to take his calls? The barriers were up before the work had even begun. It was going to be a long, hard struggle to get

Susan to agree or cooperate with *anything*. Bad news if Susan is your boss!

People buy people first

Before anyone buys into your ideas, proposals or strategies, they decide whether to buy into *you*. This includes deciding whether they will even listen to you.

Here are some of the questions your target audience might ask themselves about you (at a conscious or unconscious level):

» Do you know what you're talking about?

» Can I trust you?

» Are you just in this for yourself, or do you have my best interests at heart?

» Do you have your act together?

» Do I enjoy your company, or do you drain me?

» Do you get how the world works?

These are the types of judgements we make about others all of the time, typically based on scant evidence. As humans, we unconsciously judge a book by its cover. Psychologists call this *thin slicing*.

Every time we make a judgement like this, it shapes the way we perceive a person, and those perceptions affect the way we *feel* about them. It's in this way that, as the Japanese proverb says, 'a reputation of a thousand years may depend upon the conduct of a single hour'.

So what reputation do you create for yourself in any given moment? When your key stakeholders — the people whose cooperation you depend on to get things done — see your name pop up on their phones, or in their inbox, do they feel inclined to help or to run in the opposite direction? Do they look forward to a meeting with you? Do they view you as someone who has credibility?

CHAMPIONS OF BUY-IN DO EVERYTHING THEY CAN TO CREATE A POSITIVE EMOTIONAL RESPONSE IN THOSE THEY COMMUNICATE WITH, FROM THE VERY BEGINNING. THIS FAVOURABLE FEELING IS WHAT I CALL A *BIAS TO YES*.

Bring out your best

The list of questions in the previous section may seem overwhelming. How are you supposed to know what people are actually thinking about you? Guessing perception is a little like playing catch with a plate of jelly — it's hard to get a grip on anything. Worse still, if you start worrying too much about what others are thinking, your own confidence may start to wobble.

SO, RATHER THAN WORRYING ABOUT WHAT YOUR TARGET AUDIENCE IS THINKING, FOCUS INSTEAD ON HOW YOU *WANT* THEM TO FEEL ABOUT YOU. IN OTHER WORDS, BE *INTENTIONAL*.

Being intentional means deliberately choosing what we want others to see in us, or in other words, projecting our best authentic self. Follow the words of Shakespeare: 'Be great in act, as you have been in thought.' Your actions must align with your intent. That said, this isn't an Academy Award nomination. If you fake it, people will see through you and you'll lose all trust and credibility with them.

POSITIVE PERCEPTIONS

What version of yourself should you choose to project? What are the qualities and attributes that are most likely to encourage your target audience towards a *bias to yes*.

Take a moment to think about two or three people you know who exude a great positive influence — the type that sets them in good stead when it comes to building buy-in from you and any others when they pitch a new idea. Your champions of buy-in. How do you perceive them? What qualities and attributes do they have? What makes them effective influencers?

Table 6.1 is an example of the type of things you might come up with in doing this exercise.

Table 6.1: a sample set of perceptions

Things I admire in people who exude positive influence:		
Clear thinking	Genuine	Willing to say no
Patient	Prepared to challenge the status quo	Bring things back to big picture
Focused	See the best in others	Know their stuff
Open-minded	Selective about what they work on	Good listeners
Humble	Committed	Results-oriented

TURN THE SPOTLIGHT ON YOU

What if I were to ask your target audience to describe *you*? What words would you *like* them to come up with?

Your answer to this question represents what it means to be intentional. It provides the guiding star that will allow you to make very clear choices about what you choose to project. Without this kind of clarity, people's perceptions of you are likely to bob up and down on a sea of changing disposition.

WE ALL EXPERIENCE MOOD SWINGS; WE ALL HAVE OUR GOOD DAYS AND OUR BAD; WE ALL SAY AND DO THINGS WE REGRET THE NEXT DAY. BEING INTENTIONAL ENABLES US TO CHART A STEADY COURSE IN THE FACE OF THESE CHALLENGES.

Of course, your choice of intention will depend on who your audience is, and your objective. While one colleague might respond well to humility and empathy, another might be more positively drawn to qualities such as confidence, enthusiasm and a willingness to challenge.

Knowing your audience will help you choose your focus, but you may not always know them that well, in which case it can be helpful to seek the input of someone who does know them. Better yet, stay focused on the qualities you know serve you best in situations where you are typically at your most influential and persuasive. Simply put, bring out your best.

The three perception dials

According to behavioural scientists Amy Cuddy, Susan Fiske and Peter Glick, people socially judge others on two universal characteristics: competence and warmth. Based on their research, and in the context of this chapter, you can assume your target audience is asking themselves the following questions about you (even if only at an unconscious level):

1. **Competence.** How intelligent, skilled and strong are you?

2. **Warmth.** How likeable and trustworthy are you?[11]

Let's picture these characteristics sitting on a dial — a bit like the dials on an old-school amplifier — where each dial can be adjusted to read between zero (low) and ten (high). Now I add a third dial, which is integral to building connection and rapport:

3. **Pace.** What's the speed and intensity with which you think and speak?

73

Table 6.2 shows the *three perception dials* and some examples of the types of behaviours associated with each.

Table 6.2: the three perception dials

Examples of 'high competence' behaviours and attributes:

> » **Focusing on the technical and substantive issues**
>
> » **Demonstrating logical reasoning and thinking**
>
> » **Using confident gestures and eye contact**
>
> » **Having a strong voice**
>
> » **Appearing professional (clothes, haircut etc.)**
>
> » **Being well prepared and thorough**
>
> » **Showing strong experience, knowledge and technical expertise**
>
> » **Arriving on time**
>
> » **Presenting good written work, including correct spelling**

Examples of 'high warmth' behaviours and attributes:
  » **Showing empathy and compassion**
  » **Smiling**
  » **Acknowledging others**
  » **Using open body language and posture**
  » **Validating others' concerns and feelings**
  » **Willing to build agreement**
  » **Demonstrating humility**
  » **Using other people's names**

Examples of 'pace' behaviours and attributes:
  » **Reflective and cautious (low pace) vs quick to respond (high pace)**
  » **Using lots of pauses and silence (low pace)**
  » **Taking time to write notes during the discussion (low pace)**
  » **Sitting forward and gesticulating a lot (high pace)**
  » **Demonstrating high levels of enthusiasm and passion in voice and language (high pace)**

WHERE DO YOU SIT?

Understanding the three perception dials and the types of behaviours associated with each enables you to assess how you might be presenting to your target audience, and whether you need to adjust your behaviours to better suit that audience. Each of us has all three categories of behaviour in our repertoire, but the perception dials focus our thinking on how those behaviours show up in the context of our relationships with others.

WHAT ASPECTS OF YOUR STYLE COULD YOU 'TURN UP' AND WHAT COULD YOU 'TURN DOWN' TO PROJECT THE BEST VERSION OF YOURSELF IN ANY SCENARIO, GIVEN YOUR UNDERSTANDING OF WHAT YOUR TARGET AUDIENCE RESPONDS BEST TO?

According to the research by Cuddy, Fiske and Glick, building connection and rapport is best achieved by first projecting warmth. Once a connection has been forged, and trust established, it then becomes important to project competence. But getting the balance right can be tricky, as some contexts and relationships trigger us to fall out of balance. For example, I know that certain people will trigger me to slow right down, go quiet and look at the floor (low warmth), while others may trigger me to smile a lot and accelerate my pace (high warmth, high pace). I need to account for these default reactions by making different adjustments to my behavioural dials in these different situations.

Pace, on the other hand, is something you need to adjust to suit your audience. Some people tend to operate at a faster, more intense pace. Others present at a more cautious, reflective pace. Use the pace dial to consider how you can adjust your own pace to better match your audience's natural style. Do you need to slow down or speed up? Increase the intensity of communication or reduce it? By making these further adjustments you're more likely to increase their level of comfort, allowing for a stronger rapport.

But let's face it, it's not always easy to make these kinds of self-assessments sitting all by yourself in an office with nothing but the sound of a ticking clock to keep you company. Which is why the input of a trusted colleague or coach can be incredibly helpful here — someone whose observations you'd find valuable, or who can help you to elicit a greater level of self-awareness. You might also consider seeking the perspective of someone who knows your target audience better than you do — for example, a colleague who has had a meeting with your target audience before, and perhaps has even pitched a new idea to them.

One other point to emphasise is that this isn't an exercise in achieving the 'perfect setting' on any one of the dials. No one can tell you with objective certainty that your behaviour scores, say, a '6' on the competence dial and that you need to turn it up to a '7' to be more effective. It's far more subjective than that. Instead, think of these dials as being similar to the controls for the air conditioning: the actual number on the thermostat is less relevant than your subjective experience of whether the temperature is too cool, too warm or just right. And even when you think you've got it about right, someone else will walk into the room and tell you it's too cold!

ADJUST TO YOUR AUDIENCE

Let's look at how you can use the perception dials in practice.

Jasper is a sales executive and is about to meet with Karim, a software developer. Jasper asks Karim to consider a request to make some modifications to the settings in one of the company's online products. Jasper knows from previous dealings with Karim that he is a very technical operator and is also very reserved.

With a colleague's help, Jasper assesses the three perception dials in the context of his working relationship with Karim and rates himself as:

» Warmth: High (10)

» Competence: Low (3)

» Pace: High (8)

Karim's demeanour tends to trigger a bunch of less helpful behaviours in Jasper. For example, Jasper tends to talk way too much in the company of anyone who is more reserved, and increases his level of animation as if to compensate for its absence on the other side of the conversation (thus the high ratings on the warmth and pace dials). Jasper also recognises that he has a tendency to talk about issues at a very high level, which reflects his own intuitive way of decision making, but he knows that it can frustrate someone like Karim who wants to see the facts and figures of a business case (thus the low rating on the competence dial).

Jasper reassesses the dials and comes up with this adjustment:

» Warmth: Turn *down* — bring down energy levels, less effusive approach

> » Competence: Turn *up* — prepare more, and put something written on the table to help Karim see the rationale for my proposal
>
> » Pace: Turn *down* — speak more slowly, allow pauses for Karim to reflect and to ask questions.
>
> With these three adjustments in mind, Jasper goes into his meeting with Karim more attuned to the dynamics of the relationship and the impression he wants to project. He keeps the three dials in mind, forcing himself to slow down, drop his energy levels and meet Karim's need to spend more time examining the detail of Jasper's proposal. As a result, Jasper finds himself developing a much more comfortable dynamic with Karim — something he continues to work on in their meetings.

As in Jasper's example, using the perception dials is a matter of trial and error and continual refinement. Every relationship has its own dynamic. The three dials help you to stay attuned to the things that are likely to be contributing to that dynamic.

WHEN THE SH!T HITS THE FAN

What happens if the relationship doesn't feel like it's in sync? Despite your clear intention for the relationship, and your adjustments in approach using the three perception dials, things just aren't 'humming' the way you'd hoped.

You can't control the way someone perceives you. Their perception is theirs to own.

SOMETIMES THE MOST POWERFUL THING YOU CAN DO IS TO INITIATE AN HONEST CONVERSATION WITH A STAKEHOLDER ABOUT THE WORKING RELATIONSHIP BETWEEN YOU.

At first, this can seem like a scary thing to do. But let's not blow this up to be bigger than it really is.

At its simplest, a conversation about your working relationship is a request for feedback — an equally scary word for some! But there's a big difference between someone who makes a vague request for feedback in the vain hope they'll receive a nugget of gold, and someone who asks for feedback on the back of a really crisp intention for that relationship. Take the following two examples:

» 'I was wondering if you have any feedback for me about our working relationship?'

» 'So I've been giving some thought to our working relationship [*sharing the intent*]. It's my aim to be supportive, but I also think it's important for me to be constantly challenging you to think of things in different ways. Are those things important to you? If they are, I'd love to hear how you think it's going ...'

The first version is way too open-ended, and can leave the person being asked unsure what to say, or how honest to be, eliciting not much more than a slightly awkward, 'Umm, no, it's all good.'

The second version, by contrast, makes it much clearer what is being asked of the other person, and also makes it hard to dodge the question as the request is quite specific. It also creates an excellent opportunity to recalibrate a relationship where your intentions are misfiring.

CASE STUDY: Talking turkey

Greg was a participant in one of my workshops, in which everyone completed an exercise similar to the one at the end of this chapter. Several weeks after the workshop, Greg called to tell me he'd taken his exercise and used it as the basis for a conversation with his chosen stakeholder, Sarah, a project lead from another part of the business. Impressed by the transparency, I asked Greg, 'How did it go?'

'It took an unusual path,' Greg said. 'I started the conversation by sharing the three words I'd written down — the words that best describe the perception I'd like Sarah to have of me (in this case, *accessible, service-oriented* and *dependable*). I then asked her for feedback on how I was going with those, and she looked at me with a slightly odd frown. She then said, "I'm actually surprised by the words you've chosen. They're not really the things that are important to me at all. I mean they're all *nice*, but it's not what I'm looking for in our working relationship. They're definitely not at the top of my list."'

Greg told me that this was a huge turning point in his relationship with Sarah, because it enabled him to start focusing on the things that actually mattered to her, rather than what he'd assumed was important.

The very act of having this honest conversation was a pretty significant moment, too, in building a stronger relationship of trust.

Listen and learn

When I first started my career, I worked as a commercial lawyer. My very first boss, a senior partner in the firm, spent countless hours with me sitting alongside him, working through documents I'd drafted, ripping apart my thinking and the choices I'd made along the way. But the biggest lesson he taught me wasn't anything to do with the quality of my work, but about the dynamic of our relationship and how we communicated.

One day, as we were working through something I'd drafted, he burst out, 'Why on earth would you bore someone with all this detail?'

I sheepishly began to answer him, trying to articulate some reason to do with the importance of the detail to understanding the flow of the document. No sooner had I started to offer up my answer than he turned to me with a pained look on his face and said, 'I haven't finished yet.' I apologetically shut up, and let him continue. A few beats later, and clearly not doing a very good job of reading the play, I jumped in to respond to something he'd said, when he turned to me with the same perplexed frown, and said, 'Sorry, didn't I just say? I haven't finished yet. When I feel you've heard my point — *then* I'll be happy to hear your response!'

All this probably sounds a little more austere than it was in reality. I'd grown accustomed to his slightly eccentric style and larger-than-life personality. But I'll tell you what, that moment — and the lesson it contained — has stuck with me for a long time.

For me that lesson is the distinction between letting someone speak and making sure they *feel* heard. This is something we tend to get wrong all the time. When we think we're unheard, we're likely to feel a need to speak more loudly and more slowly. A bit like a monolingual English-speaking tourist in a foreign country who speaks more loudly so people will understand.

Ernest Hemingway said, 'When people talk, listen completely. Most people never listen.'

LISTENING IS AN ART. THERE HAVE BEEN NUMEROUS BOOKS PUBLISHED ON IT, AND THE GOOD NEWS IS IT'S AN ART THAT CAN (AND SHOULD) BE LEARNED.

While it's not my intention to delve into too much detail in this book, I do want to draw a distinction between two key forms of listening — clinical listening and engaged listening — and offer you some key tips for becoming a truly engaged listener.

CLINICAL LISTENING

Clinical listening is a skill you use when you want to get to a solution — often, quickly. It's the sort of listening you might expect from your doctor. *Does it hurt here? How long have you been experiencing that? Any other symptoms? What kind of sleep have you been getting?*

When we're in clinical listening mode we're trying to control the conversation. We want to get from A to B in the way we see fit, often within a limited timeframe. As a result, we tend to filter out everything that seems extraneous or irrelevant to that pathway, and our listening reflects our desire to keep things on track. Follow-up questions are often used to steer the conversation in the preferred direction. *What happened then? Did you speak to Bob? Who told you to do that?*

Clinical listening has an important role to play when our sole purpose is to solve a problem. Say, for example, a team member comes to you and asks you to identify whether they've left anything out in preparing a report to the Board. A few precise questions — such as, *Did you reconcile this data with Steve's set?* or *Are you planning to include this information as an appendix to the full report?* — might enable you to get to the nub of any issues and provide a clear answer quickly.

But we very easily default to clinical listening even though the situation may call for a greater level of connection with the other person. This is especially relevant in the context of building buy-in, which requires us to build the kind of relationship in which others feel heard and understood.

ENGAGED LISTENING

Engaged listening is aimed at building connection and rapport. Sure, information will be exchanged in the process. But more than anything, engaged listening creates a feeling in your target audience that *they* matter.

For some, the idea of engaged listening will seem painful, especially when your only interest is to get a job done, but engaged listening is often the key to unlocking resistance.

> AFTER ALL, BUY-IN IS NOT ABOUT HAVING THE RIGHT ANSWER; IT'S ABOUT HELPING PEOPLE GO WITH YOU ON A JOURNEY. POOR LISTENING CAN BE THE VERY THING THAT CAUSES RESISTANCE.

As renowned author Stephen R. Covey says, 'The real beginning of influence comes as others sense you are being influenced by them — when they feel understood by you — that you have listened deeply and sincerely, and that you are open.'[12]

TOP FOUR TIPS FOR ENGAGED LISTENING

So what does it take to be an engaged listener? To listen to others in a way that helps them to hear you? Here are my top four tips to help keep you in engaged listening mode.

Tip 1. Be curious, not incredulous

Engaged listeners listen with a curiosity to understand the other person. That means suspending judgement or the desire to convince the other person that they're wrong. This can be hard to do when you have your own, perhaps opposing opinions, or when your ego wants you to show everyone how smart you are as early as possible in the conversation. That's why it helps to have some standard questions or phrases you can use to stay in curious mode, even when instinct is pulling you in a different direction. Here are some of my personal favourites:

- » Why is that?
- » Help me to understand that …
- » Talk me through that …
- » I'm curious to understand what you mean when you say …

Here's a little game to play with yourself: Imagine you're about to play the role of your target audience in a movie. Do you understand the way their mind works? Do you really get their thinking? Do you appreciate why they do the things they do? This can help you to shift to a whole different type of listening.

Tip 2: Listen out loud

One fundamental of engaged listening is that it gives the speaker a sense of connection — where your full understanding of what they've told you brings them closer to you, so they feel they can trust you that little bit more than before.

One way to do this is to listen out loud. This can serve as a great prompt for them to keep going, but it also sends a strong message that you are genuinely thinking through everything they say. It also gives them an opportunity to correct you if you're wrong.

Here are a few examples of what 'listening out loud' might sound like in practice:

'Oh, okay, so you're probably thinking that's going to cause you difficulties down the track?'

'As you speak, I can really sense the frustration.'

'That's hilarious!'

'Ah, I see, so you're finding it hard to reconcile this project with the broader strategy?'

'Oh, wow!'

Another important effect of listening out loud is that it can serve to validate the other person. Psychologists often talk about validation as a powerful aspect of good listening, as it gives the other person the sense that their voice is legitimate and worthy — a key to building connection and empathy.

Tip 3: Listen to the great unsaid

Engaged listening is also about listening for unspoken information — things they're not saying explicitly, but can readily be gleaned from their tone of voice, demeanour, pauses, facial expressions and so on.

SO MUCH OFTEN REMAINS UNSAID IN CONVERSATION, AND THE MORE YOU CAN DO TO DEMONSTRATE YOUR SENSITIVITY TO THE UNSPOKEN STUFF, THE MORE LIKELY YOU ARE TO BUILD REAL CONNECTION THROUGH YOUR LISTENING.

Take the following conversation between two colleagues. Person A is leading a project and is asking person B to come on board as a contributor:

A: Did you have any questions about the overall aims of the project?

B: Um ... no, not really.

A: (Wondering whether B's hesitation is a sign of something) Where do you sit with it?

B: Oh, look, I don't necessarily have a view. (A notices that B isn't making eye contact with her and is shrugging his shoulders in a resigned way.)

A: (Gently) Is it that you don't have a view or you don't feel it's worth sharing it here?

B: Oh, look, clearly this is going to happen whether I like it or not, so you just tell me what you need me to do.

A: It sounds as though you've got some concerns about the project, and I'd love to hear about them. What's troubling you?

At every beat of this exchange, A is responding to what B has *not* said, rather than his words. This is where the *real* listening happens. So long as it's done gently and without bullying the other person, this kind of listening can be an important way to build connection and empathy.

Tip 4: Be careful what you don't say

Similarly, there's a lot you 'say' to the other person through the non-verbal aspects of your listening. How do you listen with your face? With your eyes? With the way you position and move your head, body and arms? Tone of voice? Don't misunderstand me: this is not a call for dramatic mime. In fact, there's probably nothing more distracting than someone sitting across from you having a private facial expression party.

When I'm listening intently, I have a tendency to frown. This has got me into trouble on more than a few occasions, as people mistakenly assume I am sitting there thinking to myself, 'What rubbish!' Which is not true (well, most of the time).

Ask a friend or coach to offer you observations about the things you do when you're listening and how those things might have an unintended impact on the person speaking.

Another valuable exercise is to film yourself having a conversation with someone (with their permission, of course), then watch it back. You'll probably cringe on the first viewing. It's a natural reaction, but when you watch it the second or third time, you'll start to notice things about how you conduct yourself in the conversation.

After the first viewing, turn the sound off and watch it in silence. What do you notice about your non-verbal language? What do you do with your eyes and your face? Your head? Your arms and hands? Your posture and body movements? It's amazing how much you can pick up from seeing yourself in video footage, because it's not a perspective we typically have of ourselves.

Make them look good

Theatre improvisers have a mantra: *make your partner look good.* This philosophy sits at the core of strong ensemble work. Improv shows can very quickly fall apart if one performer is prepared to trample all over the other performers to get their own moment in the spotlight. This can fly in the face of instinct for many performers, who are often in it for the stage time, but the best improvisers serve the overall scene or show, not their own ego. And if that means staying out of a scene — or a whole show — so be it.

This is an incredibly valuable principle to live by when it comes to building buy-in.

NO MATTER HOW GOOD YOU MIGHT THINK YOUR IDEA OR INITIATIVE IS, THE ONLY THING THAT MATTERS WHEN IT COMES TO BUY-IN IS HOW YOUR AUDIENCE FEELS.

They need to feel important, and that their opinion and ideas matter. Nothing will undermine this more than letting your own ego and desire to be 'in the spotlight' take over, which is a little like being taken to a karaoke bar by someone who clearly enjoys singing more than you do, only to find yourself dragged up on stage and forced to sing along with them. Urgh.

There's a big difference between those who make others look good, and those who make themselves look good. At the heart of the distinction lies a willingness to be humble. Perhaps you recall the images of Pope Francis, crouched on his knees, washing the feet of twelve prisoners on the first Holy Thursday after his election? For a man who had just ascended to the highest position of authority in the Catholic Church, it was an act that said to the world, *What's status got to do with anything?* This was a sublime embodiment of what it means to be humble.

A great example of a leader who makes others look good is Howard Schultz, the previous CEO and chairman of Starbucks. Schultz emulates what is often termed *servant leadership* — a style of leadership that Schultz himself describes as 'putting others first and leading from the heart'.[13] As a highly successful businessman, presiding over a monolithic brand with an arguably plentiful pool of potential employees, Schultz could well have been the kind of CEO who chose to lead from the ivory tower. But, to the contrary, Schultz is known for listening to his employees and prioritising their needs. He makes others look good, and feel good. Which perhaps explains why his own staff gave him a 91 per cent approval rating on US jobs website glassdoor.com.

So follow Schultz's lead: choose to make others look good. And here's all you have to do:

» Respect and acknowledge someone else's effort and contributions.

» Give credit where credit's due.

» Acknowledge their experience, expertise or status.

» Address them by their first name, make eye contact and smile.

» Express an interest in their point of view ('I'd love to know what you think … ').

Or, to put it all far more simply, treat people the way you'd have them treat you.

Over to you

Pick a specific person — someone who is, or is likely to be, your target audience for a particular idea or initiative.

1. What are three words you would like them to use to describe you? What kind of impression would you like to leave them with?

2. What are you already doing that you believe would lead them to associate these three words with you? What are you doing that might be incongruent with these words?

3. What are two or three words you'd hope they don't use to describe you? What are you doing (or not doing) that might cause them to have that negative view of you?

4. What behaviours can you focus on to clearly project the qualities you identified in question 1, and to avoid the negative perceptions you identified in question 3?

5. Rate yourself using the three perception dials on how you interact with this person. You might like to ask a friend or trusted colleague to help you.

6. What adjustments can you make to any of the perception dials to create a stronger sense of connection with the other person?

* * *

You've spent this chapter under the spotlight. When it comes down to it, people buy people first, so we've looked at some of the things you can do to ensure people feel a *bias to yes* when they interact with you. Throughout this first part of the book we've been busily getting set for success, and now you're probably well and truly ready to pitch your idea. So, let's do it …

Part II
Go

The groundwork is laid. All that effort you've put into getting set for success is about to pay off. It's time to put your idea in front of your target audience — to get heard and take them on the journey from 'what do you want?' to 'yes, I want in!'

The path to yes is an unpredictable one, but in this second part of the book, you'll discover a powerful model to navigate your way along it. The 3M model has three parts to it:

» **MOOD.** The heart tells the mind where to focus its attention. Feelings fuel our willingness to listen and to act. Unless our target audience is in the mood for yes, buy-in is going to be an uphill slog.

» **MIND.** Give me a business case, show me the data. Does it all add up? Their logical mind has a decision to make and it needs your help.

» **MOVEMENT.** Buy-in is nothing but a happy vibe unless there's action to back it up. Champions of buy-in don't just shape mood and minds — they engineer action.

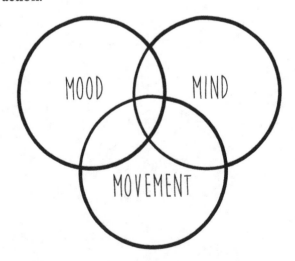

CHAPTER 7
MOOD
Make them feel it

'What your heart thinks is great, is great.
The soul's emphasis is always right.'
Ralph Waldo Emerson

When you put your idea on the table does it excite people, scare them, inspire them or perhaps confuse them? Is their gut instinctively crying out, 'This feels right, let's do it!' Or is it screaming, 'Oh God, no ... Taxi!'

You've surely been in situations where you're presenting an idea and your audience:

» aren't listening or, if they are, they're disengaged (is that the sound of crickets chirping?)

» don't care in the same way you do — or worse, couldn't care less

» struggle to remember what you've just presented to them

» are distracted by other priorities or messages on their smart phone

» look at you like you just ran over their cat.

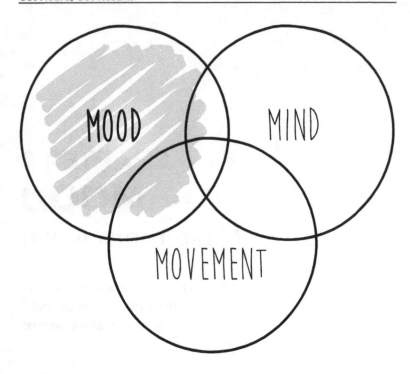

These are all symptoms of one key problem: your audience is just not *feeling* it.

Capture a feeling

A dark-haired man with chiselled looks drives along a rugged coastline in a convertible, the top down and his companion's long golden locks blowing in the breeze. The sky turns from blazing red to burnt orange to ochre as the sun dips into the sparkling blue ocean. He turns to the girl and smiles, a deep loving smile. His eyes sparkle with the reflection of the sunset. She tilts her head back, laughs and throws her arms into the air in exhilaration as they accelerate into the distance …

Clichéd? You bet. Yet this is an image that car commercials have been using for decades. Why? It captures a *mood*. It stirs up *emotions*. It makes you *feel* something. *Happy. Carefree. (Okay, maybe even sick.)* No matter how posed or fake your rational mind insists this image is, it's one that works. It sells cars.

'Yeah, but that's a TV ad. That's not how it works in real life.'

The world of advertising may seem a tenuous comparison to draw when it comes to the nuanced world of building buy-in among colleagues, managers and customers. After all, ads tend to portray a pretty distorted view of reality, and are often primed towards manipulating impulsive behaviour that defies all logic (I admit, I've been there, I once purchased a steam mop from a late-night shopping TV channel) — none of which will get you far in building strong, trusting relationships.

But ads are a proper field trip for those of us seeking to connect with an audience, to capture their heart and trigger an instinctive urge for everyone to jump up onto the boardroom table yelling, '*Let's do it!*' when we present them with an idea.

Advertising has a clear purpose that goes well beyond merely offering information to viewers: ads are designed to build an emotional connection between you and a brand, so when you are in the store at the moment of purchase you'll select the brand you feel warm and tingly about, rather than the unfamiliar, two-dimensional competition.

CAPTURING THE HEART ISN'T SIMPLY ABOUT GRABBING PEOPLE'S ATTENTION. ONCE WE EMOTIONALLY CONNECT TO SOMETHING, WE'RE PREPARED TO INVEST IN IT — AND ACT.

In fact, the stronger that emotional connection, the harder we'll work to come up with compelling, logical reasons to take action (as when I had to justify the steam mop purchase to my wife).

When you ask people to buy into an idea or proposal, you're trading in their future. You're asking them to invest in something that is *yet to happen*. The logical part of their brain will assess the pros and the cons. *Will it work? What will it cost? What are the risks?* These are all questions that matter — on paper. Meanwhile, as our cognitive computers click and whirr into action, at an unconscious level we've already been asking ourselves, *Yes but, how do I feel about this?* It is the heart that decides what the mind will focus on.

Make up your mood

Emotion plays a significant role in every decision we make. We might tell ourselves or others to 'keep emotion out of it', but work by Antonio Damasio, professor of psychology, philosophy and neurology at the University of Southern California, suggests this isn't possible. In his book *Descartes' Error*, Damasio observes that our brain is hardwired in such a way that whenever we make a decision, we're taking our cues from emotion.[14]

SO THE ACT OF MAKING A DECISION *IS INEXTRICABLY TIED TO* EMOTION.

Not only that, but the way we feel affects *how* we make a decision. Certain emotions — called 'high arousal emotions' — make us more prone to take action, while other 'low arousal' emotions cause us to hesitate or become apathetic. High arousal emotions include surprise, amusement, excitement and awe, as well as less pleasant feelings like anger, fear and frustration. In contrast, low arousal emotions include the feeling of being relaxed, serene, content, sad or bored.[15]

So how does all this impact your ability to build buy-in? If you're trying to get others to jump on board with your idea, to see your initiative as one they want to get involved with, then you need to make them feel an emotional pull towards your idea. A *bias to yes*, much like the bias they feel when they think about you.

Shape their mood

Start by asking yourself this simple question: what do I *want* my audience to feel? What emotional frame of mind do I want them to be in as I present my idea to them? Without the right feeling, everything else will be hard work, a little like trying to grow a vegetable garden in arid soil.

This is not an invitation to manipulate or practise sorcery. It's about identifying a feeling that reflects the way *you* feel. To fake a feeling would be like filling a room with some kind of buy-in gas while strapping on an oxygen mask so you don't succumb to its effects. Do this quick honesty test: if your target audience stopped you on the street and asked, 'Are you trying to make me feel [insert emotion here]?', could you look them in the eye and answer with complete conviction, 'Yes I am, because that's how *I* feel about it'?

Of course, you can't *control* other people's feelings, nor should you ever try to, but there are five strategies you can use to help shape their mood and create a *bias to yes*:

1. Project the mood.
2. Share stories.
3. Use metaphors and similes.
4. 'Zap' them.
5. Get extreme.

Let's look at each of these in more detail.

1. PROJECT THE MOOD

Bernadette, a senior sales manager, was preparing a speech to some of her company's key customers in which she was going to launch some important changes to one of the company's products. As I watched Bernadette practising her speech, I didn't feel anything. It was just information, a bit like reading an instruction manual out loud. I stopped Bernadette and asked her, 'How do you want me to feel right now?' After a pause, and a few moments of looking perplexed, she responded: 'Intrigued.' I suggested to Bernadette that she repeat what she'd presented, this time projecting a sense of intrigue.

The presentation suddenly came alive. Bernadette assumed the stance of someone who was sharing a secret with me. She started to use expressions like, 'I want to share something with you' and 'Let me give you a sneak peak at something my team has been working on long into the night'. I couldn't help but smile. It was a complete transformation that left me feeling, well, intrigued.

IF YOU WANT PEOPLE TO FEEL RELAXED, THEN BE RELAXED. IF YOU WANT PEOPLE TO BE INSPIRED, SHOW THEM HOW INSPIRED YOU ARE. IF YOU WANT THEM TO BE CURIOUS, BE OVERTLY CURIOUS YOURSELF. LEARN TO BE INFECTIOUS. LEARN TO *PROJECT THE MOOD*.

The mood you want to project has to ooze from every pore. It has to infiltrate every aspect of how you present your idea. A cute one-liner, or simply saying, 'I'm excited,' isn't going to do the trick. People need to feel the mood from the way you:

» introduce your idea and describe your *Big So What* (from chapter 3)

» exude energy as you enter the room

» set up the environment (the mood of the room) you're in

» convey your tone of voice

» use body language and facial expressions.

It's hard to project a strong mood across all of these aspects unless you well and truly believe in your idea. This is why catalysts have the upper hand when it comes to buy-in. If you're not feeling it, then go back to chapter 3 and your *Big So What* for guidance.

I think very carefully about how I'm going to project the mood each time I facilitate a team session or run a workshop. No matter how focused I am on the content of a session, or the needs of the audience, I make a conscious choice at the beginning to set the right *tone*. I play some carefully chosen music to lift the mood. I joke and clown around with people; I use self-deprecating remarks to show them it's okay to be wrong. I get people to do things like help me to shuffle furniture around, getting rid of tables and asking people to bring their chairs over to a different part of the room. All of this is disarming, but it also sends a subtle signal to participants that this is not a typical day at the office; we're getting ready to think and do things differently.

It's amazing to watch how this can very quickly shift the energy in the room. People start to talk to each other, laugh and connect, all of which puts them in a much better frame of mind to consider the ideas I'm about to put in front of them.

Once you see your target audience engaging, the effects on your own energy and emotional state can be significant. When they look interested, you feel more compelled to share. When they sit forward, you feel more drawn to them. When they nod in recognition of your point, you feel encouraged to go on. But remember, you're getting all these powerful cues back from them because you put in the effort to foster the right mood and tone from the outset. Get it right, and that energy will build momentum and fuel the entire conversation.

Top tip

Do you sometimes find yourself swinging from one meeting to the next like a monkey? The energy from one conversation can bleed into the next, affecting your mood and how well you present your idea. I regularly see executives walking into meetings with the air of someone who has just gone three rounds with Muhammad Ali—which might be how they're feeling after a week of hard work and internal stakeholder battles, but it's not doing them any favours in setting the tone with their audience. That kind of negative energy drags everyone down. You're supposed to be a catalyst, remember!

Actors often take a moment after a rehearsal or an exercise to 'shake it off'. Shaking it off involves literally a big shake of your body to throw off the emotion and feelings of whatever you've just been doing. If this feels uncomfortable or downright weird in the middle of the office, then try finding a quiet space, closing your eyes, taking a deep breath in and then allowing yourself a big exhale. Visualise the negative energy leaving your body, and imagine the positive energy and the right mood you want to project in your next meeting. Open your eyes and step into this new state.

2. SHARE STORIES

According to Gabrielle Dolan, storytelling expert and author of *Stories for Work*,[16] 'As human beings, we are hardwired not only to share stories but to listen to stories — it's what we do. Through a story you help the listener visualise and feel something. Stories tap into an emotion that helps the listener make a connection to your story that they will most likely remember, because the fastest way to the head is through the heart.'

Storytelling is an incredibly powerful way to evoke an emotion in your audience. Stories resonate with people's real-life experiences, memories and imagination. Even the expression 'Let me tell you a story ...' can be enough to make us lean forward in our chair and drop our guard.

In his book *Generating Buy-In: Mastering the Language of Leadership*, Mark S. Walton focuses on the role of strategic stories as the single most important way in which leaders bring people on board with their ideas. As Walton explains, 'We "think" in stories. Stories, filled with pictures — images of life — are literally the language, the currency of our minds.'

In fact, research demonstrates that by using evocative language, stories can trigger sensations in us that mimic the real thing. Consider the evocative power of a few simple words — 'a perfect summer afternoon' — and the places it takes you. Our imaginations are literally the hub of virtual reality! Walton concludes, 'The age-old secret to generating buy-in is to strategically design, target and deliver a story that projects a positive future.'

But there is a big difference between telling a story to your friends or family and telling a story in a business context, including when you're building buy-in. Dolan adds, 'When it comes to using stories in business, there is a real discipline and skill required. It can't be self-indulgent. It needs to be purposeful, appropriate for your audience and, most importantly, authentic.'

Feel the pain

A well-told story can allow your audience to feel a problem and an empathic response. Not long ago, a client told me how she had used the following story to win the support of her management team to adopt a more creative approach to flexible working arrangements:

> It was 2011. I'd just been appointed to a senior executive role in the company where I'd been slogging my guts out for the last six years. The selection process had been ruthless and I felt a mixture of exhaustion and relief. I went home that evening to share the news with my family. As we sat together around the dinner table, my six-year-old daughter said to me, "Mummy, does the new job mean you'll be happy now?" Taken aback, I turned to her and said, "Darling, what makes you think I'm not happy?" And she innocently responded, "Because you have to rush to work every day and you're always grumpy, and then you're grumpy when you come home too. Your work doesn't sound like fun." It was then that I realised I'd completely lost all perspective. I'd let my career hijack my life.
>
> So what did I do? Well, I didn't go in the next day and give my notice. I didn't move to the seaside. I kept the job but made a decision: from that point on, I would make it my leadership challenge to build a culture where people could be their best at home and at work. In fact, a culture where people could just be their best.

It's hard not to picture the moment in this story when the young daughter asks the golden question. It's a moment that transports the audience to that dinner table — a bit like the movie camera of life just zoomed in for a serious close-up. As a result, my client's management team felt the problem, and became far more open to change.

Opportunity knocks

If used well, stories can also allow your audience to sense the opportunity you're presenting to them. Such stories can be as short and simple as this example from Jeff Bezos of Amazon: 'There are two kinds of companies, those that work to try to charge more and those that work to charge less. We will be the second.'

Or they can be more elaborate, such as this example, a paraphrased version of a presentation I watched the CEO of a digital services client deliver to a group of staff, while responding to their concerns that the company's new strategy was too aggressive:

Three years ago, I stood up in front of everyone and laid out our three-year strategy. There were some huge targets in there. And I'm going to let you in on a little secret: I was terrified. I went home that evening and asked myself, can we really do this? Have we stretched too far? But each day, I would tell myself, we're either all in or not in at all. We either choose to be number one, or we may as well go home. I learned what trust means, what it really means to hire the best people and then allow them to exceed all expectations. The result is now part of our history. We smashed it. Not only did we hit our three-year goals, we exceeded them. You guys rewrote the playbook for the whole industry! We proved to ourselves that we are capable of amazing things when we harness our energy. Well, I guess our new strategy is asking, who's up for the next challenge? We're about to go into the next phase of our growth. We face new challenges; the market's changed enormously and will keep changing before our very eyes. But you know what? I couldn't feel more confident that, three years from now, we'll be sitting here again, celebrating the fact that we've been able to maintain pole position.

What I love about this example is that it channels a story of past achievement and projects that story into the future. This is also a great example of projecting a mood.

WHAT THE CEO PRESENTED TO HIS TEAM WAS A SENSE OF PRIDE, ACCOMPLISHMENT, DARING AND EXCITEMENT. IT INFECTED HIS AUDIENCE. THEY JUMPED ON BOARD.

The gentle art of storytelling

Using stories to help build buy-in and create the right mood is an art and a skill. While there are plenty of resources on the topic (and I'd highly recommend you explore them separately), here are my top five storytelling tips:

» **Give it purpose**
Why are you telling the story? What's the purpose? What do you want them to do/say/feel when you finish? Nothing loses people faster than a story that leaves them asking, '*Huh? What's that got to do with anything?*' One way to test your purpose is to finish with the line 'So why am I sharing this story with you?' (a bit like 'and the moral of the story is ...').

» **Be authentic**
Tell stories that matter to you. It's a common theme throughout this book, but telling stories that you don't truly believe in yourself is a fast track to breeding cynicism and breaking trust.

» **Be relatable**
Tell the story in a way that your audience can put themselves into it. The person in the story — whether it's you or someone else — has to be someone people can empathise with or relate to. The story above is relatable because the CEO shares his own fears and challenges. He takes his audience on a human journey that everyone can relate to.

» **Keep it simple**
It's easy to get lost in a story, to fly off on a tangent, to fill your stories with extraneous details and information that don't serve the purpose or the audience's experience in any way. But less is often more. Keep the point of your story clear and simple. Leave plenty of room for people's imaginations to start creating a picture. Be like Coco Chanel, whose rule was always to look in the mirror before leaving home and remove one accessory.

» **Project the mood**

Finally, it's worth noting that the earlier advice of *project the mood* applies in spades when it comes to telling stories. Are you telling a story or simply sharing some information? There's a big difference, the most important of which is that the former is all about evoking a mood. The mood you project when telling a story is a little like the soundtrack in a movie. Relish the moment of telling the story and inject it with the energy of *giving*. Make eye contact with your audience and show them you really want them to hear your story. Don't rush it; take the time to reflect on the key moments of the story.

3. USE METAPHORS AND SIMILES

While stories are a powerful way to evoke your audience's feelings, they take a bit more time to construct, learn and deliver with effect. Metaphors and similes, however, are a shortcut to achieving a similar effect.

Metaphors and similes act as comparison points. They help your audience to understand one thing by comparing it to something else they're already familiar with. 'Your bedroom is a pig sty' or 'Reading this report is like wading through *War and Peace*'.

Metaphors and similes are like emotional portals, allowing you to access the subconscious mind of your audience by tapping into their past experiences. By hitching a ride on an idea that's already familiar to them, you're not just helping your audience to make sense of your idea, but also evoking a corresponding feeling.

'Hello, I'm a Mac.'

'And I'm a PC.'

Perhaps you remember those opening lines from an ad campaign run by Apple from 2006 until 2009?[17] These ads were designed by Apple to highlight all the reasons why a Mac is better than a PC — in a humorous way so people would actually *enjoy* watching them — but they also personified the PC and the Mac. Apple used a very powerful metaphor of individual style and identity. The audience was left to ponder: which one of these two *people* am I?

In the American version of the ads,[18] 'PC' was portrayed as a slightly chubby man wearing an ill-fitting suit, conservative glasses and an immaculate old-school hairstyle. 'Mac', on the other hand, was a cool, bohemian guy. The metaphor conveyed a strong message to the audience about the *real* difference between the two brands — one that cut to the core of personal identity — fueling the long-running Mac versus PC debate in a playful, teasing way.

A clumsily chosen metaphor or simile, though, can leave your audience feeling confused and disengaged. Until recently, when we started to examine the role of mood and feelings in building buy-in, I used to announce to my workshop participants that it was 'time to get on your Barry White'. Much to my disappointment, I've found that there are a number of people in my audience who have never heard a Barry White song. This reference was often met with a sea of blank faces, and one day someone even asked if I was talking about 'that real estate agent'. I felt like I was throwing out my most comfortable pair of slippers (yes, another metaphor), but Barry had to go.

Similarly, overused or clichéd metaphors can leave your audience feeling queasy rather than inspired. Standing in front of a group of people and saying, 'We need to go into battle and fight for our survival' may evoke a battlefield image for you, but it's been done to death. The same can be said for, 'It's time to play the game on our terms and reclaim our position at the top of the ladder'.

The lesson here?

CHOOSE YOUR METAPHORS FOR YOUR AUDIENCE, NOT FOR YOURSELF. CHOOSE SOMETHING YOU KNOW THEY CAN RELATE TO – BUT IF IN DOUBT, KEEP IT OUT. A METAPHOR SHOULD NEVER NEED EXPLAINING.

4. 'ZAP' THEM

Will Rogers once said, 'There are three kinds of men. The ones that learn by readin'. The few who learn by observation. The rest of them have to pee on the electric fence for themselves.'

To build buy-in effectively, you often have to let your audience come into contact with the electric fence. That is, let them experience the problem that your idea will solve, or the opportunity you're proposing. This is what I call 'zapping' your audience.

Car salespeople know this when they get you into a car as quickly as possible; auctioneers tap into this when they run an auction in front of the house they're selling. Steve Jobs was famous for his live demonstrations of new products on stage, so the audience could *experience* the new Apple product. Apple's worldwide retail outlets are designed in the same way, giving customers the chance to be 'hands on' with each and every product.

If a picture is worth a thousand words, a firsthand experience can tell the whole story. A client of mine used this to her advantage when she had to transform the large bank she worked at into an activity-based workplace. The whole idea of an active workspace is that you move desks every day, so when the initiative was first announced, most staff reacted negatively to the idea they would no longer have a desk and chair (let alone their wall of dog photos). To address this, a simulation centre was set up where team members could spend a week experiencing the method first-hand. The reaction after a few days was, 'You know, that wasn't so bad after all.'

Letting people get 'zapped' shows you are confident and honest.

IF YOU GIVE YOUR AUDIENCE THE CHANCE TO EXPERIENCE THE REAL THING BEFORE MAKING A DECISION, YOU'RE EFFECTIVELY SAYING, 'DON'T TAKE MY WORD FOR IT. COME AND SEE FOR YOURSELF. IF YOU DON'T LIKE, DON'T BUY-IN.'

And who can argue with that?

If you don't have the luxury of a hands-on experience, try other ways to simulate the real thing, as Luke did in the following example.

CASE STUDY: Game on

Luke, the manager of a sales team, had been trying to get his team to attend a series of lunch-and-learn sessions that he'd coordinated, the aim of which was for participants to exchange learning experiences with one another. But as much as he tried, Luke struggled to get people to attend. Digging deep, Luke decided it was time to 'zap' his team. One Monday afternoon, as the team prepared for its weekly sales meeting, Luke set up the meeting room to resemble the set of a game show. As the last of the team members arrived, Luke declared, 'Let's play!' He immediately described a customer situation and asked two of the team to step up and role play how the conversation could unfold, while inviting some of the other

---

team members to act as the judging panel (complete with scorecards à la *Dancing with the Stars*).

The game was a lot of fun, but it also proved to be a clever strategy for building buy-in, because it gave people the opportunity to see the kinds of things that their colleagues were doing, and also to feel the pain of realising they didn't have the best answer for every situation. Attendance at the lunch-and-learn sessions skyrocketed.

5. GET EXTREME

Sometimes you've got to throw a glass of icy cold water into people's faces to get their attention. Well, not literally, but you can use language and actions to take people completely by surprise.

It's an extreme — and sometimes risky — strategy to confront your target audience with statements that reflect your message and are deliberately brazen, but it can grab their attention and provoke them into action.

Take a look at the following examples:

- » 'We are all so damned comfortable. That comfort is killing us.'
- » 'Some days I wish I could work for the competition. Because we are making their job so damned easy.'
- » 'Our team has lost the plot!'
- » 'Today I'm placing an all or nothing bet on our strategy.'
- » 'I've got a confession to make that I may live to regret ...'
- » 'We are on a conveyor belt to irrelevance. Today I'm asking all of you to hit the "emergency stop" button.'

Each of these statements is likely to cause an audience to look up from their Twitter feeds and at least wonder what the heck you're talking about.

CASE STUDY: Vinomofo

One company that knows what it means to *get extreme* is popular Australian online wine retailer Vinomofo. In a crowded market, Vinomofo stands out not simply for the deals it offers customers, but for its brand and the mood it projects. Vinomofo is prepared to *get extreme* — from its name, which stands for 'wine motherf**ker', to the ballsy language it uses. For example, one of its most common sayings is 'Forget the bowties and bullshit'.

This isn't the work of some hip, over-caffeinated copywriter sitting at company HQ. It reflects the true style and personality of the company's founders, including Andre Eikmeier. In one of Eikmeier's blog posts, he writes:

> **Why is it that so many of us are crippled by overwhelming confusion, stripped of our mojo, as we step through the winestore doors, approach the cellar door counter, or open the restaurant winelist? So much so that we dive for the nearest lifeline, a familiar red Penfold's logo, or some bloated Marlborough buoyancy vest. Anything we recognise as "safe" amidst the stormy seas of confusion.**
>
> **It's not your fault, it's — the industry. I already went there with that "stormy seas of confusion" schmaltz, for those of you still reading :)**

The thing that makes Eikmeier's approach leap off the page is that he clearly stands for something, and he's prepared to throw rocks at the rest of his industry — and no doubt has ruffled some bowtie-wearing connoisseurs along the way. After all, you've got to be prepared to make someone uncomfortable when you get extreme.

DATA TO BE DIFFERENT

Another way of going extreme can be through the way you present data and what might otherwise be drab information.

Al Gore went extreme with the data in his movie *An Inconvenient Truth*. At one point in the movie Gore presents a graph to demonstrate the link between fluctuating carbon dioxide levels and the Earth's temperature over the past 650 000 years. As Gore approaches the present day, he climbs into a scissor lift — the graph spikes so high, Gore needs the lift to stand alongside its peak point. Then, as the graph projects forwards to forecast the next 50 years, Gore continues to extend the height of the scissor lift until he's right at the top of what is a very large screen. It was a dramatic and memorable way to make an otherwise cerebral data point.

Celebrity chef Jamie Oliver went to similar extremes in a presentation he gave at the 2010 TED Global conference.[19] Oliver was highlighting the increasingly high levels of sugar in the diets of children in America, setting his sights on flavoured milk as a major culprit. To illustrate his point, Oliver tipped an entire wheelbarrow of sugar cubes onto the stage, declaring it to represent 'five years of elementary school sugar, just from milk'. Oliver pointed to the pile of sugar and went on to declare, 'Now I don't know about you guys but ... any judge in the whole world would look at the statistics and the evidence and they would find any government of old guilty of child abuse.' It was an extreme moment, both in the visual stunt and his language, both of which matched the impassioned and at times angry mood Oliver was projecting throughout his speech. The audience broke into applause, clearly moved by the moment.

A word of caution, however. Be careful if using any extreme strategy.

WHAT YOU BEGIN WITH SHOCK-AND-AWE NEEDS TO BE MATCHED WITH SUBSTANCE, OTHERWISE YOU RISK CONFUSING (OR WORSE, LOSING) YOUR AUDIENCE.

There's no point making a brazen statement that bears little or no resemblance to the truth. Announcing, 'I've had enough of same same. It's time to flip this company on its head', and then outlining a strategy that feels, well, *same same* isn't going to impress anyone.

If overused — or abused — the *get extreme* strategy becomes the classic case of the boy who cried wolf: no one will listen next time.

SURPRISE!

A milder version of 'get extreme' is to say or do something unexpected. This can create interest and surprise, making it a powerful way of triggering a mood in your audience — especially when the prevailing mood feels as though it's not serving your objectives of gaining people's buy-in.

Not long ago I was on a Virgin Australia flight bound for Brisbane. The cabin crew launched into the safety demonstration — something frequent flyers like myself tend to ignore simply because we've been subjected to it so many times. In truth, we haven't heard it all before. Every plane (as the cabin crew always says) is different, and every airline mixes it up. But we *assume* we know it all. We've become desensitised to hearing the same messages over and over a … zzzzzz. On this flight in particular, the flight attendant making the announcement decided to mix things up. On introducing us to our life jackets (not that I was listening), she said (and now I was), 'The whistle is for attracting sharks. The light is so you can tell us all how big the shark is. It'll be quite the party.'

In this case, the flight attendant's quip got everyone's attention, but more importantly had everyone smiling (except the odd person who wasn't sure if she was for real). She'd tilted the mood. I found myself craning my neck to see if I could see her. I couldn't as she was too far away, but I knew one thing: I liked her style.

Over to you

1. *Make up your mood:* Think of an idea or initiative you're currently working on and write down the words that best describe the mood and feeling you want others to have when they hear about your idea.

2. *Shape the mood:* In your example, identify the ways in which you can:
   » project the mood
   » share stories
   » use metaphors and similes
   » 'zap' them
   » go extreme.

* * *

In this chapter, we've explored a number of powerful ways in which you can create the right mood for buy-in. The right mood sets the scene for your target audience, draws them in as you're pitching an idea or initiative and fosters a *bias to yes* in their hearts. Once you have them hooked, it's time to move on to the next dimension in our 3M model: Mind.

CHAPTER 8
MIND
Give them a reason

'The mind is not a vessel to be filled but a fire to be kindled.'
Plutarch

The mood is set. Your audience's hearts are thumping in heady anticipation. They're *feeling* a bias to yes, so why aren't we done yet?

Trying to secure buy-in on the basis of mood alone is like trying to drive with the handbrake on. We might 'feel' like saying yes, but our rational thinking brain is in the driver's seat and it's looking for signs that this is logically the right move to make. This is the world of *Mind* — the second dimension of our 3M model.

To draw on a metaphor used by Chip and Dan Heath in their wonderful book *Switch: How to Change when Change Is Hard*, our emotional, intuitive side is like a huge elephant, while our rational, logical side is the person riding the beast. 'Perched atop the Elephant, the Rider holds the reins and seems to be the leader. But the Rider's control is precarious because the Rider is so small relative to the Elephant. Anytime the six-ton Elephant and the Rider disagree about which direction to go, the Rider is going to lose. He's completely overmatched.'

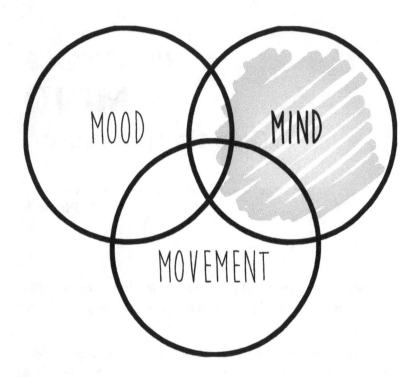

The Rider might be small in relation to a six-ton Elephant, but it asks the tough questions and keeps us from making poorly thought through, impulsive decisions — or at least, tries to. It's the Rider who works out how to deal with complex problems that make progress hard, the sorts of things that might otherwise scare the Elephant into running away.

Of course, the Rider doesn't always get a say. We often do things based purely on intuition and emotion — sometimes for good reason (asking someone out on a date), and sometimes to our regret (losing our temper with a colleague or a loved one).

When I decided to start my own business, the Elephant was well and truly awakened. I was emotionally biased towards a resounding 'Yes!' But for over a year I hadn't actually made any progress on doing anything about it. What was slowing me down? I kept saying to myself, *Don't rush into this Simon, work through the detail.* The logical, rational side of my brain insisted that I do the sensible thing and carefully work through the pros and cons, trying to find a way to manage the risks, calculate the cashflow, determine the best timing — and so the list went on. It was a big decision and one my practical brain wasn't ready to commit to, no matter how much I felt like I wanted to.

That's why buy-in involves a mood–mind connection. *Feeling* and *logic* have to work together, to be ready to play on the same team, in order for us to say 'yes'.

Syncing mood with mind

As much as we like to be inspired by the things we do, it's hard to justify risky decisions on the basis of mood alone. Imagine your CEO standing in front of hundreds of shareholders, announcing that the company will be opening offices in a new city just because 'It *feels* right, don't you think?'

Plato described emotion and reason as two horses trying to pull a chariot in opposite directions. While that's how it can sometimes feel, neuroscientists tell us that the two sides of our brain act in elegant concert with one another.

EMOTION HELPS US TO KNOW HOW TO ACT ON LOGICAL CONCLUSIONS, AND LOGIC HELPS US TO MANAGE OUR EMOTIONS.

The challenge when building buy-in is to *align* our audience's logical thinking with the way they feel about our idea. This is particularly important in the business world, which places an enormous premium on logic and sound decision making, which is magnified by the multiple layers of managers and owners all looking to scrutinise every decision made.

THE LOGIC OF 'YES'

When you ask someone to buy into your idea or initiative, their rational brain calculates furiously whether it's a good idea or not. *Is it worth it? Is it a smart idea? What's the value? Where's the proof?* By working through these types of questions, they are seeking to arrive at a rational answer — what I call a *logical yes*.

Let's look at the two primary ingredients of a *logical yes*.

WHAT'S IT WORTH?

What is the value of a stand-up desk? How about a set of measuring cups? A leaf blower? A kilo of arabica coffee beans?

If you're searching your brain for the price tag of these items as they might sell in a shop, then you're looking in the wrong place. 'Price is what you pay; value is what you get,' said world-renowned investor Warren Buffett. So how do we define the value of an idea?

HERE'S THE TRICK: HOW VALUABLE *YOU* THINK YOUR IDEA IS DOESN'T MUCH MATTER WHEN IT COMES TO BUY-IN. THE ONLY THING THAT MATTERS IS WHAT *THEY* THINK — THAT'S THE PEOPLE YOU'RE TRYING TO ENGAGE, YOUR TARGET AUDIENCE.

Like beauty, value is entirely in the eye of the beholder. One person's prized antique is another person's doorstop.

At the risk of dampening the mood with an equation, value can be expressed as:

Value = Benefits - Cost

Benefits means all the ways in which your proposal or idea is good for me — the extent to which it meets my needs and drivers, and gives me satisfaction. As I sneak in a cheeky donut for morning tea, the benefits seem clear: aside from sating my appetite, I get to feel a sense of indulgence and enjoyment.

Of course, I know there's a *cost*, aside from the cash I just handed over. I can't seem to get the fabulous line 'A moment on the lips, a lifetime on the hips' out of my head. Donut confessions aside, the cost of your idea includes anything I need to give up or suffer in return for accepting your proposal. That may include risks I take on, inconvenience, diversion away from other activities, time away from family, for example.

Put yourself in your target audience's shoes: how might they see the value of your idea or initiative? In particular, ask yourself the following questions:

» What would make this an idea worth investing in? What are the real benefits to them?

» What concerns and reservations are they likely to have? What are the costs to them?

» How can I address these concerns, or how flexible am I willing to be to modify my idea or proposal to address their reservations?

» What questions do I need to ask before I can fully appreciate and understand their perception of value?

In giving thought to these types of questions, you will begin to see value not through your own eyes, but through theirs. *That* is the key to building buy-in.

PROVE IT

Even if I see value in what you're proposing, how can I be sure it will actually work? What would other people say? Will I look stupid for saying yes? How will this look if it ends up in the news? Getting your audience to a *logical yes* means helping them to address these kinds of questions.

VALUE IS A HIGHLY SUBJECTIVE THING; PROOF, ON THE OTHER HAND, IS FAR MORE OBJECTIVE. PROOF IS ANCHORED IN THE OPINIONS OR EXPERIENCES OF OTHERS – IDEALLY, PEOPLE WITH THE RIGHT KIND OF EXPERTISE AND WISDOM.

People derive proof from a variety of sources, such as:

» research and data, numbers and statistics

» case studies and examples of how your idea has worked elsewhere

» testimonials, online reviews and ratings that show what others think

» verification from consultants and experts.

The business world trades heavily in proof or evidence. It enables executives to show their key stakeholders that risks are taken on only where it's objectively smart to do so. Proof not only gives your audience assurance and confidence that it's wise to proceed, but also helps them to feel that they've covered their backside in the event things go pear-shaped.

In the late 1980s there was a saying bandied around the IT world: 'No one ever got fired for buying IBM.' This wasn't just a marketing slogan; it was an axiom invented by customers themselves. Consumers loved buying IBM because the proof that the product worked was overwhelmingly on their side. *We can rest easy knowing that we've made a smart decision.*

It's a wonderful thing when proof becomes a part of your brand. This holds true for all of us. Our own track record ultimately becomes the greatest form of proof we can offer.

DON'T FAKE IT TO MAKE IT

Mark Twain once famously wrote, 'There are three kinds of lies: lies, damned lies and statistics.'[20] The fact is, numbers and statistics can often be massaged to prove even a weak argument. An even worse version of this kind of transgression is to, well, make it up. To hint that there *is* proof when in fact there is none may be tempting, given this 'proof' will often go unchallenged.

Just don't do it.

GETTING PEOPLE ON BOARD IS NOT SIMPLY A MATTER OF CONVINCING PEOPLE TO SAY YES. IT'S A MATTER OF GENERATING GENUINE, VOLUNTARY COMMITMENT. THIS REQUIRES PEOPLE TO INVEST IN YOUR IDEA AND IN YOU.

The moment you get caught playing make-believe in the world of proof, however innocent that little white lie might seem, is the moment that trust collapses, bringing with it all your hopes and dreams for buy-in.

Make sure you do your homework. Prepare to show your audience proof and evidence they may genuinely need to see to support your idea. Ask yourself these questions:

» What data or other evidence am I relying on?

» What assumptions am I making about their relevance to my own idea or proposal?

» How can I best share my sources of proof in a way that allows my audience to fully understand my thinking and reasoning?

» What other sources of proof might my audience have seen, or might they want to see?

CREATE, DON'T FABRICATE

Of course, proof may not always be available to you. Perhaps your idea is unique and so new that there's nothing to point to. What do you do then? You *create* proof — which does not mean you fabricate proof! Conduct your own mini-laboratory or research experiment that enables you to establish proof of whether or not your idea will work.

Companies engaged in rapid innovation do this all the time: they practise a 'test and learn' philosophy. This kind of approach accepts that truly innovative ways of doing things will lack solid proof, but that shouldn't prevent the company from at least giving it a try.

Take, for example, global online travel company Expedia. According to former CEO Dara Khosrowshahi, the company's test and learn culture is based on the notion that, 'regardless of how senior you are, if you have an idea, it will get tested and live or die based on that'.[21] With this kind of approach, the proof, as they say, is in the pudding.

This can be especially powerful when done in collaboration with your target audience. Consider asking them, 'What's the simplest way we can test the merit of this idea so you and I can make a decision about whether to take it further?' Even in situations where you have brought established proof to the table, switching to this kind of collaborative approach can work well to keep the conversation moving.

Go slow to go fast

> *'Go wisely and slowly. Those who rush, stumble and fall.'*
> **William Shakespeare**

Now you've thought about what value you're offering to those you're seeking buy-in from, and prepared the proof that will help convince them that your idea is a smart one, it would be easy to think you've got buy-in in the bag. *All I have to do now is swoop in, stick a pen in their hand and ask them to sign on the dotted line, right?* ... Wrong.

You may be sold on your idea, but your target audience is still at first base ... if they've even stepped onto the field yet.

Your job is to help them move along a path of thinking that allows them to see the value and the proof in the same way you do. But they will have questions. They'll have doubts. They may need time to think things through, to voice objections, to think some more, to spit the dummy, to sleep on it overnight and then change their mind. That all takes time. If you try to fast-track that process, the risk is that they become suspicious of your agenda or disengage from the whole idea. None of us likes the pushy salesperson. We all have finely tuned 'foot in the door' detectors.

YOUR JOB IS TO ESCORT YOUR AUDIENCE ALONG A PATH OF LOGIC THAT ALLOWS THEM TO JOIN THE DOTS THEMSELVES. *GO SLOW TO GO FAST.*

At the same time, you can't afford to allow things to drift aimlessly on a cloud of indecision. You need to drive their thinking towards a conclusion — even if in some situations that means a 'no'.

To guide you along the path to a *logical yes*, figure 8.1 (see overleaf) shows five sequential steps to follow.

STEP 1: EXPLAIN

This is your opportunity to open the conversation about your idea with a clear and compelling explanation. Knock 'em out with your conviction! Demonstrate the *Big So What*. Set the right mood and tone. Show them the value and the proof. Now is the time to put into practice all the crucial elements you've learned so far in this book to get heard.

Make sure you are specific and clear. This is not the time for fluff. Nothing clouds the path to a *logical yes* more than ambiguity. There's a big difference between 'I'm seeking to create a more innovative culture' (*Okay ... so what do you want from me?*) and 'I'm asking every team in the business to participate in a half-day workshop designed to identify how we as a business can become more innovative'.

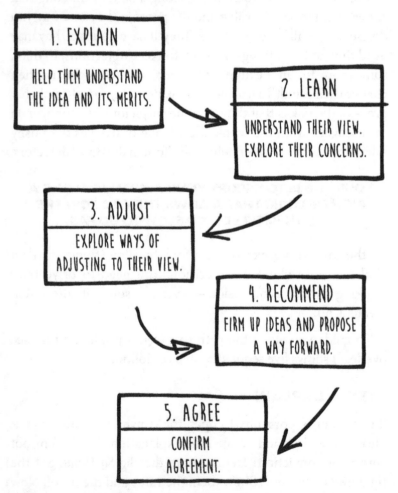

Figure 8.1: The Path to a Logical Yes

Part of the art here is to distil your explanation to the most salient points. As a basic rule, you need to get to the second step — *Learn* — as quickly as possible. So ask your audience if anything is unclear and if they need you to explain more, rather than drowning them in detail they don't need at the outset.

Your goal in this first step is not to get your audience to actually agree to anything (yet) — only to present your proposal in the best possible light before you hand the metaphorical microphone to them. Remember, this is only the first of five steps. Less is more! Aim to get to the next step as quickly as possible because, chances are, your audience can't wait to have their say.

STEP 2: LEARN

All that matters in this second step is what *they* (your audience) think. Set aside your ego and let them talk. Remember our tips for engaged listening in chapter 6? Now's your chance to listen like a pro and learn from them. Kickstart the conversation by asking lots of questions:

» 'What are your initial thoughts?'

» 'How does this sit with you?'

» 'What do you like about the proposal? What don't you like?'

» 'What's your view on the value of an idea like this?'

» 'What are your concerns?'

Then ask plenty of follow-up questions to keep the conversation going. Your aim is to gain as deep an understanding as possible of your audience's perspective so you know where they stand on your idea. This is going to help you to make any necessary adjustments at the next step in our sequence.

Embrace the 'black hole'

It's highly likely in the second step that you'll start to see some pushback and resistance from your target audience. I call this the *black hole*. It's filled with the fears, reservations and concerns that are playing out in the minds of your audience as they think about your proposal. You can feel the black hole sapping the energy from a conversation, sucking any chance of a 'yes' into the ether.

YOUR FIRST OBJECTIVE IS *NOT* TO 'NEUTRALISE' THE BLACK HOLE, BUT TO *UNDERSTAND* IT. THE KEY IS TO ACKNOWLEDGE YOUR AUDIENCE'S FEARS. TO ADDRESS THE BLACK HOLE, HEAD ON.

You might say something like, 'I imagine there are all kinds of questions running through your mind about how this would work, and perhaps some concerns. I'd be really keen to hear what those are. I know if we don't address those now, then it will be difficult for you to get on board with this project.'

Keep asking questions until it seems they've run out of things to share (often the momentum builds as they get going, so for a short but scary time it may feel like a runaway train). Once you feel as though there are no questions left to ask and they've shared all there is to be shared, the best thing you can do is summarise the conversation to date and ask them whether there's anything you've missed. Use phrases like 'Let me check I've understood everything you've raised so far …' then confirm you're on the same page by asking whether there's anything you've missed.

The abrupt 'no'

What happens if you're faced with an abrupt and explicit 'no' in the first or second step? You might feel like packing up your suitcase and going home (or throwing it out of the window), but it's too early to know for sure.

While 'no' can *feel* like an immediate shutdown, it's important to maintain a *what's possible?* attitude (which we explored in chapter 2). Assume for a moment that they have good reason for saying no, and that you've completely missed a beat. Adding the letter 't' to their monosyllabic response can help you to imagine that 'no' is simply an incomplete version of:

» *not* today ...

» *not* in that form, because ...

» *not* unless ...

» *not* until ...

» *not* as long as ...

IN THE FACE OF AN ABRUPT 'NO', SIMPLY *IGNORE AND EXPLORE*. IN OTHER WORDS, IGNORE THE PRESENTING 'NO' OR COUNTER-DEMAND, AND INSTEAD REMAIN FOCUSED ON UNDERSTANDING *WHY* THEY'VE SAID NO. STEER A STEADY COURSE AND EMBRACE THAT BLACK HOLE!

STEP 3: ADJUST

The third step is to explore how you might adjust your proposal to address your target audience's concerns and unmet needs.

As tempting as it might seem, the aim here is not to resolve everything they've raised in one go. Nor is it to assume that you will be able to come up with a neat solution to everything in one fell swoop. To do this would be putting far too much pressure on yourself.

Besides, there is tremendous power in taking the time to allow your target audience to contribute ideas for addressing the objections or concerns they've raised. Don't assume that they even want you to come up with a tidy solution to all of their fears.

Your attempts to solve things too quickly may deprive people of the very thing they need: an opportunity to work through their concerns, to have a voice in how your idea is implemented and to feel heard and understood.

If you put them into the seat of troubleshooter (rather than troublemaker) you allow them the chance to be the hero in this conversation. Let them be part of the exploration. If they do come up with a solution then it's more likely to make them a raving fan of your work — always a good thing when it comes to buy-in.

Here are some questions you might ask at this step:

» 'You mentioned this would cause confusion in the marketplace. How do you think we can avoid that? I'd love to hear your ideas.'

» 'The last thing either of us would want is to have our team working on the wrong things in the wrong order. Did you have any ideas about how we could overcome that?'

» 'We established earlier that there may be a skills issue that would make it hard to get this project off the ground. Here's what I'd propose to mitigate that risk ... Can you see that working?

» 'I fully understand your concern ... If we do go ahead with this, what would it need to look like to get around that concern?'

STEP 4: RECOMMEND

This step is where your audience begins to adopt a stance of 'Okay, this *could* be something I *might* be willing to agree on ...' They may say something along those lines to you, or they may give the air of someone who no longer has any major reservations or concerns. Either way, you're looking for signs that the black hole has receded into the distance.

The aim here is to table a clear version of your idea or initiative for their buy-in. In other words, this is where you finalise a proposal for people to say 'yes' to.

How about this ...?

It's at this point that you need to pull together the threads that have emerged from the previous three steps, and drive the conversation towards a *logical yes*. There are two ways to do this:

1. **Make a recommendation yourself.** Based on what you've learned, and the adjustments you've explored together with them in steps 2 and 3, you might now say something like: 'So, based on what we've been discussing, here's what I'd like to suggest ... '

2. **Ask them to make a recommendation.** This is a little more risky, as it's putting the ball in their court. But it can be an incredibly powerful moment if they play. You might say something like, 'So let's see if we can pull this conversation together into a concrete next step. How would you recommend we go about this?'

Even though both of these are framed as questions, it's important to imbue this step with a little more forward momentum. Keep an eye on the energy levels of the conversation, and don't be afraid to unleash your catalyst and step into a bit more of a leadership role. For example: 'How's this for a suggestion: why don't we run a pilot event next week and invite one person from each of the management groups, and then use that as an opportunity to refine our approach? Are you happy if we run with that?'

If they are still hesitating — or perhaps even showing outright resistance at this stage — you know you've probably tried to move things forward too fast, in which case you might need to rewind the tape back to step 2, *Learn*.

Hint at implementation

As you start to drive the conversation towards agreement (step 5), you might also begin to explore questions around implementation. Questions such as these:

» When would be the best time to start?

» How long do we need to secure budget for this?

» Who else needs to be involved?

» What's the best first step?

In fact, this aspect of buy-in corresponds with the third dimension of our 3M model, *Movement*, and is the focus of the next chapter. But touching lightly on this conversation as part of the *Recommend* stage is a great way to test the waters around your target audience's readiness to move into the final *Agree* stage.

More than anything, exploring implementation helps your target audience (and you) to make an important shift: a psychological shift from 'this is just an idea' to 'this is something we're serious about doing'. This triggers a shift into very different thinking gears, and it can also evoke a different emotional response that either helps you to build positive momentum ('I can't believe we're actually going to do this — how exciting!'), or it can highlight that you need to slow things down a little ('Hang on, I just don't feel comfortable about this ...').

IT'S LIKE STANDING AT THE OPEN DOOR OF A PLANE AT 10 000 FEET, HAVING MADE THE INITIAL DECISION TO GO SKYDIVING WHILE IN THE SHELTERED COMFORT OF YOUR HOME.

STEP 5. AGREE

After patiently guiding the conversation through the first four steps, you're now at the point of tying it all together — turning ideas and discussion into agreement and commitment. With a nod to the title of that classic book on negotiation, it's time to *get to yes*.

So are you in or are you out?

In the world of professional selling, they tell you to *ask for the business* — the part many people forget or skirt around. People awkwardly and fearfully bale midway through the conversation, simply because they're scared that after all this hard work they might not get a clear 'yes'. To quote Peter Cook, co-author of the book *Conviction: How Thought Leaders Influence Commercial Conversations*, 'If you have something of value, something that could change this person's life, that could make their world better, and you've both spent an hour with the express purpose of determining whether this is for them, and you want to work with them, ask for the business. Make the invitation. If you don't, you have wasted both your time and theirs ... You've brought them to the brink, you've shown them a new possibility, a different future, and then you've yanked it away from them.'

> **IN THE CONTEXT OF BUY-IN, 'ASKING FOR THE BUSINESS' EQUATES TO ASKING FOR THEIR SUPPORT. NOW IS THE TIME TO SEEK A 'YES'.**

You can do this by asking one of the following types of questions:

» 'Can I have your support on the basis of what we've discussed here today?'

» 'So are we all on board with the following proposal?'

» 'Are you happy to proceed based on everything we've discussed here?'

» 'Is that a "yes" from you?'

This is when the champion of buy-in surrenders to the merit of their proposal. At this point, it's all about the value and proof as your audience sees them. If you've done your work throughout the preceding four steps, then you'll have done everything you can to paint the right picture around both of those elements. Now let those things be the deciding factors. Don't confuse the moment as one in which they might accept or reject *you*. They are now making a fully informed decision about how they feel about the overall merit of the proposal, and unless you've rushed things, it's unlikely there's much more you can do to influence that view.

On the flipside, asking for a 'yes' prematurely *is* something to be wary of, because chances are you won't have done enough to ensure the best chance of success at this point.

Pick your moment

In chapter 5, we explored the importance of timing (remember, it's the secret of comedy and the key to catching a surfable wave).

THE TIMING WITH WHICH YOU ASK YOUR AUDIENCE FOR THEIR AGREEMENT IS CRUCIAL. RUSH IT AND YOU MAY GET KNOCKED BACK SIMPLY BECAUSE THEY FEEL PRESSURED. ALLOW THEM TOO MUCH TIME AND THE MOMENT MAY BE LOST.

So how do you know when to ask? Well, there's no simple answer to that question, but there are two things to consider. First, if the moment is brimming with signals that read, 'I'm in, I'm in', then seize that moment. To return to my surfing analogy from chapter 5, don't miss a good wave when it comes.

The second consideration is whether it is useful to ask them for clearance. You might say something like, 'Well, given where we've got to today, I'd be very keen to know whether I have your support. How are you feeling at this point? Do you need any time to consider?' If their answer to this is yes, then the next thing to do is lock down the time when you will reconvene. For example: 'That's absolutely fine. How about I revisit this with you in a week's time?'

The underwhelming yes

On 13 December 2015, the French foreign minister Laurent Fabius sat in front of an auditorium filled with hundreds of political dignitaries from around the world and declared, 'I see the room, I see the reaction is positive, I hear no objection. The Paris climate accord is adopted.' He then added, 'It may be a small gavel but it can do big things.'[22] And so Monsieur Fabius closed the global climate change conference in Paris, and world leaders forged an international accord to curb man-made greenhouse emissions. As the sound of the gavel echoed around the chamber, ministers stood up to cheer and applaud loudly. The deal was done.

But not every scenario will result in the kind of spontaneous applause and celebration unleashed by the French minister's gavel. Sometimes buy-in comes with a small or underwhelming yes. Perhaps they shrug their shoulders, nod slightly and say something like, 'Ummm, okay, I guess so.' And you're thinking to yourself, 'Oh for goodness sake, is that the best you can give me? What's the problem *now*?'

Top tip

In his book *Getting Past No*, William Ury talks about people's need to save face in negotiation, particularly if agreement requires them to make a significant move away from their initial position. This is equally true in the context of building buy-in. Take some time to step into the shoes of your target audience, and consider how they might be feeling about the journey they've just embarked on.

The champion of buy-in knows when it's time to embrace the first yes — even if it's a guarded one — and treat it as an opportunity to get the wheels in motion and build some momentum. Think back to when your target audience stepped onto the path — right back at the Explain stage. What was their demeanour then? And how does their current state compare with that?

If you've managed the journey along the path to yes with empathy and sensitivity, then you will have given them plenty of space and opportunity to make the transition. You will have helped them to feel heard and done what you can to tailor your idea to account for their concerns.

YOU WILL HAVE MADE IT YOUR PRIORITY TO ENSURE YOUR AUDIENCE SEES THE VALUE AND PROOF IN YOUR PROPOSAL BEFORE ASKING THEM TO BUY IN.

All of these things will have been instrumental in getting to this point: a *logical yes*. And, if the Mood is right, you now have a willing heart and a willing Mind. Wow … congratulations!

But don't be fooled into thinking that your work is done — that it all somehow stops here. Quite the reverse, this is where it all begins. After all, as Pablo Picasso once said, 'Action is the foundational key to all success.'

Over to you

1. Think of an idea or initiative you're seeking buy-in for. How can you best articulate the value it offers to your target audience? What are the benefits of your

idea in their eyes? What proof or evidence do you have, or can you identify and provide, that will help build their buy-in?

2. What's the black hole in your example? What fears, concerns or reservations do you think they will have about your idea?

3. How will you address those concerns as you follow the five steps to guide your audience towards agreement (Explain, Learn, Adjust, Recommend, Agree)?

* * *

So there you have it, the second dimension of our 3M model, *Mind*. We've been exploring what it takes to guide your target audience towards a *logical yes*, helping them to establish value and proof. We've seen how important it is to go slow to go fast, and to allow your audience plenty of opportunity to voice their concerns and to have a say in the final outcome.

Everything in this book so far has been a step along the journey of creating buy-in. With Mood and Mind in sync, perhaps your target audience is finally declaring, '*Yes, I'll work with you. Deal!*'

Now's the time to explore how to turn that 'yes' into action.

CHAPTER 9
MOVEMENT
Convert to sustained action

'A journey of a thousand miles begins with a single step.'
Lao Tzu

Be honest now, did you skip ahead to this chapter at some stage thinking: Movement? That's what I'm after. Lights, camera, action — I'll go straight there!

Or perhaps you got to the end of the previous chapter and thought: *Great, we've got the 'yes' we were after. Surely now I can relax and pop the champagne. I'm done, right?* ... Sorry, but you couldn't be more wrong.

Both of these are common pitfalls when it comes to the gentle art of buy-in. Either we try to push things along and move too quickly as a result (remember the mantra from chapter 8: 'go slow to go fast'), or we hear the 'yes' we've been working so hard to achieve and assume all our work is done.

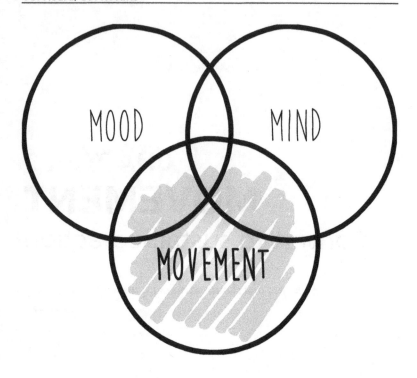

Perhaps you've been in a meeting, presentation or part of a conversation where there's been an overwhelming sense of positive spirit in the room, where everyone has sat earnestly nodding and declaring their enthusiastic support for an idea. Then, only days later, you find yourself standing in the corridor feeling the cold wind of inertia tickling your face, wondering what on earth is wrong with everyone? *Why aren't people doing what they said they would do?*

It's one thing for people to *say* yes, but it's quite another for them to act on it, even with the best intentions. To quote Johann Wolfgang von Goethe, 'Thinking is easy, acting is difficult, and to put one's thoughts into action is the most difficult thing in the world.'

Aside from the fact that there's a litany of forces working against us — bloated to-do lists, over-crammed schedules and rigid systems, not to mention the prevailing conditions we explored in chapter 4 — we're also pretty fickle creatures when it comes to staying on task. Willpower simply isn't all it's cracked up to be, especially when it all stinks of hard work. The status quo is such a comfy sofa: *why do today what you can put off until tomorrow?*[23]

CHAMPIONS OF BUY-IN UNDERSTAND THAT AGREEMENT AND COMMITMENT ARE SIMPLY THE PLATFORM WHERE THEIR REAL WORK BEGINS.

What good is having people emotionally and rationally on board but failing to take the very action you need from them in the first place? Without the third dimension of our 3M model, *Movement*, all of your diligence to this point will have been hard work for naught.

Become a master of movement

With a little discipline and ingenuity, you can find a way to 'hack the system', to overcome the human tendency to dwell in delay, and instead become a master of making movement happen.

It starts by following two key principles:

1. Talk action.
2. Talk accountability.

PRINCIPLE 1: TALK ACTION

Champions of buy-in make implementation and action a part of every conversation they have. They don't just enjoy the high-five moment associated with getting that big 'Yes!' Before closing a conversation, a champion of buy-in will invest the additional time to ask, 'So how do we make this happen?'

Champions of buy-in don't just cross their fingers and hope everything will work out as planned. They bring forward some of the tricky questions around what's going to get in the way. They don't pretend those things won't exist. They know they have to tackle them.

When I practised as a commercial lawyer, clients would often raise the question, 'What happens if the other party to the contract doesn't do what they said they would do?' and I was regularly astounded by the number of times a lawyer acting for one of the parties would respond, 'We'll make sure there's a watertight dispute resolution clause in the contract. If they renege we'll take them to the cleaners!' A clever, legal response, I'm sure, but how does that help anybody fulfil the intent of the agreement or deal they're doing in the first place?

In a *Harvard Business Review* article titled 'Getting Past Yes: Negotiating as if Implementation Mattered', negotiation expert Danny Ertel wrote, 'People who view the contract as the conclusion and see themselves as solely responsible for getting there behave very differently from those who see the agreement as just the beginning and believe their role is to ensure that the parties involved actually realize the value they are trying to create.'[24] While Ertel may have been writing here about negotiation, his observations are no less true in the context of getting people's buy-in to anything.

Taking the cue of experts in this field, influencing as if implementation matters requires us to take the time to pose some questions:

» What happens next?

» What will it take to progress towards implementation?

» What's likely to get in the way or slow us down?

» How can we overcome these obstacles?

» What can we do to tip the balance in favour of action rather than inaction?

» What can each of us start doing immediately to take this agreement forward?

» What does each of us expect to see happening that's different as a result of today's conversation?

» Where to now?

AS A RULE OF THUMB, SPEND AT LEAST HALF AS MUCH TIME AGAIN DISCUSSING IMPLEMENTATION AS YOU SPENT NUTTING OUT THE AGREEMENT ITSELF.

PRINCIPLE 2: TALK ACCOUNTABILITY

It's one thing to talk action and implementation; it's quite another to ensure each person in your target audience knows their role in it.

Ending every conversation with a clear understanding of *who* is taking *what* action, and *when* they'll have it done by, is a key ingredient in getting this right.

In many instances, even a willing target audience will look for opportunities to hedge their bets when it comes to taking action. It can be tempting for people to create for themselves a safe harbour of ambiguity, just so they have the option of not delivering down the track. Your job is to eliminate any of those safe harbours so people can't hide in them.

This becomes especially important when your target audience comprises multiple people — say, a team or a diverse group of stakeholders. In these contexts, it's far too easy for everyone in the team to enthusiastically express buy-in ('Yes, let's do it!'), but then not do anything about it themselves ('I thought that was Bob's responsibility ...').

Say, for example, a team agrees that they will do more to engage with different stakeholders across the business, to get better quality feedback about a product under development. But when, two weeks later, no one in the team is able to report taking any positive steps towards this new and important goal, the team's manager is likely to feel confused and frustrated.

If, however, at the end of the meeting, the manager asks each individual to respond to the question, 'What's the one thing each of us will do as a result of today's discussion?', the manager could be a lot more confident of action occurring. Even better, the manager could ask each individual to declare their commitment somewhere highly visible. For example, using Post-it notes collected on a flipchart sheet of paper, and placed somewhere visible on a wall. Or on an online forum or discussion board. This creates relationships of accountability between members in the team, which helps to build a culture of inter-accountability, reducing the team's dependence on the manager as the 'accountability police'.

The three phases of Movement

Learning to *talk action* and *talk accountability* will dramatically increase the likelihood of converting agreement into action. Champions of buy-in apply these two principles across three phases of Movement (see figure 9.1).

START $\implies$ SCAFFOLD $\implies$ SUSTAIN

Figure 9.1: Three Phases of Movement

1. **Start.** How do you get those critical first steps to happen?

2. **Scaffold.** What can you do to ensure that there is enough support and infrastructure in place to keep people on the right path?

3. **Sustain.** How do you create action or change that lasts the distance, becomes sustainable and goes beyond the initial enthusiasm?

START

Every project has to start somewhere. You want a beautiful vegetable garden? You have to prepare the soil first. You want people in your team to start using a new data management system? They have to know how to log into the system first.

No matter how good an idea, and how enthusiastic your target audience may be to bring it to life, getting started can be the hardest part.

Here are three useful strategies you can draw on to overcome inertia, tackle the barriers to beginning and get your target audience to take those first steps in the right direction:

1. Start small.
2. Choreograph the dance moves.
3. Throw a 'starty party'.

1. Start small

Ever seen a croquembouche? It's one impressive-looking cake — a towering pyramid of choux pastry puffs, each filled with *crème pâtissière* and dipped in crispy caramel, the whole thing then shrouded in a veil of spun sugar. Stupendous.

If asked to make one, most people would go a little pale. The cake looks terrifyingly complex. But, in fact, when you break down the recipe, it's a fairly simple thing to make. So long as you take it one step at a time: 'Place the water and butter in a saucepan. Bring just to the boil. Remove from heat and use a wooden spoon to beat in flour until combined.' Do that much and you've just ticked off the first step. Look at all 17 steps at once, go a little dizzy.

NOTHING INHIBITS ACTION MORE THAN BEING OVERWHELMED BY THE SHEER ENORMITY OF THE TASK. BY BREAKING A TASK OR PROJECT DOWN INTO *TINY CHUNKS*, STARTING SMALL AND TAKING ONE STEP AT A TIME, IT BECOMES MUCH LESS LIKELY THAT YOUR TARGET AUDIENCE WILL FREEZE IN TERROR.

When I ask my kids to tidy their room, the prospect of going into the bedroom and cleaning up their toys is one that sucks the energy out of their bodies (and admittedly mine also). However, if I set a highly visible timer on my iPad[25] (or better still, I get *them* to set it) and say, 'Let's go crazy for the next three minutes, and see how much we clean!', suddenly the task ahead doesn't feel so enormous, and it might even be fun. In fact, it often happens that my kids end up pleading to add another minute or two to the timer.

Top tip

I used the *tiny chunks* method regularly when writing this book. I started off using what is called the 'Pomodoro Technique', which suggests that you work in 25-minute bursts of energy with a five-minute break in between. No matter what mood I'm in, the idea of writing for 25 minutes without stopping isn't too scary.

One sales team I worked with found that everyone in the team needed to set up an additional three meetings per week in order to get the kinds of results they were after, which in turn meant making an extra ten phone calls per week. At first, the initiative stalled — until the manager broke it down into tiny chunks. She said, 'This week, let's all make two more calls than we would normally do: one before lunch on Tuesday, one before lunch on Wednesday. I'll check in with each of you before you head off for lunch that day.' *Everyone* did their extra calls. By starting small, the manager had made it almost impossible to fail. The next week, she upped the target to four additional calls, the week after eight, and the week after ... you guessed it: sixteen.

Another way to help keep the first steps small is to frame everything as an 'experiment'. If your target audience is daunted by the scale of a task, try proposing a 'small experiment' as a way of getting things started. For example: 'Let's test the idea by each asking one stakeholder for their reaction this week, and then reporting back in our weekly meeting. Who knows what they'll say — it'll be an interesting experiment.' This not only gets people thinking small, but also allows people to leave their perfectionist tendencies at the door, and just try something.

2. Choreograph the dance moves

'It's a jump to the left; and then a step to the right. With your hands on your hips, you bring your knees in tight ...' Anyone who grew up dancing the 'Time Warp' — from *The Rocky Horror Picture Show* — not only knows the moves, they can describe them to a tee. The famous lyrics provide the clearest choreographic instructions you can possibly hope for.

When it comes to buy-in, consider how you can provide your target audience with similarly crisp guidance as to what you need them to do. It's one thing to get a team of managers to agree to provide more feedback and coaching to their staff; it's quite another to provide them with clear, practical advice on what that should actually look like. In the absence of that clarity, there's a real risk that people will sit around, paralysed by analysis, waiting for the 'perfect moment' to provide that feedback to their staff.

To counter this risk, take the time to really define what it is they need to do in terms of action. Consider how you can choreograph the dance moves with the same kind of clarity as the 'Time Warp' song.

CASE STUDY: Wipe off 5

Few people would argue the importance of road safety — and driving at safe speeds is a key component of that. While most countries have speed limits, studies have shown that many drivers believe it's 'safe' to drive a little over the speed limit, which has led to the phenomenon of 'low-level speeding'.

In August 2001 the Transport Accident Commission (TAC) in Victoria, Australia, launched a campaign designed to reduce the incidence of people exceeding the legal speed limit, even by small amounts. To do this, the TAC's campaign got very specific: it asked drivers to 'Wipe off 5'.

'Wipe off 5' is a good example of a choreographed dance move. The emphasis on Movement — asking drivers to check their speedo and reduce their speed by 5 km/h — was something that had been missing from previous campaigns, where the focus had been exclusively on Mood and Mind.

The result? The 'Wipe off 5' campaign was acknowledged as a key contributor to a drop in speeding at the time, as well as road death and injury rates.[26]

3. Throw a 'starty party'

Getting started can feel intimidating. One way to neutralise that anxiety is to throw what I like to call a 'starty party'. A starty party is an event where the emphasis is on taking action together and having fun while doing it — a little like a fun run. Running may not be something many people ordinarily think of as 'fun', but the idea of getting together with others on a group run clearly has a motivating effect on many runners — otherwise, it wouldn't have become a global phenomenon.

Not only does the fun run leverage the power of the group but it usually creates a playful vibe, with loud music, group warm-ups, stalls and prizes. In other words, it feels like a party, even though everyone's about to slog their guts out pounding the pavement.

A similar phenomenon is the 'hackathon', which has taken the tech world by storm. It's essentially an intensive group event where people (such as designers, programmers and other IT wizards) get together — surrounded by pizza and caffeine — and smash out new ideas and projects.

THE PRINCIPLE IS SIMPLE: HARNESS THE POWER OF COLLABORATION WHILE SHARING AND HAVING FUN.

Australian tech megastar company Atlassian is famous for its quarterly ShipIt days, where 'Atlassians' are given the opportunity to take an idea or a problem, assemble a team and go crazy on developing a solution for 24 hours. The best ideas get implemented in the business.[27]

The principle of the hackathon can be applied to any project or initiative: embrace the idea of bringing people together, create a feeling of intensive but playful collaboration — and watch progress happen.

SCAFFOLD

With the first steps of your idea or project underway, the real challenge becomes keeping people on the straight and narrow, maintaining the agreed behaviour or staying focused on the end goal.

SCAFFOLDING THE CHANGE IS ABOUT CREATING A KIND OF 'INFRASTRUCTURE' AROUND YOUR TARGET AUDIENCE THAT MAKES IT HARD FOR THEM TO CHOOSE ANYTHING BUT THE DESIRED OR AGREED BEHAVIOUR.

Good scaffolding reduces dependence on fickle qualities like self-discipline and willpower. Scaffolding sets things up in a way that makes success more akin to 'colouring by numbers'.

As a champion of buy-in, *you* are the most important form of scaffolding. Once you have people on board, the hard work is to keep them there, particularly when the going gets tough. This means you need to remain highly vocal and visible throughout the initial phase of creating movement. As you seek to build momentum, you need to be the cheer squad, providing lots of encouragement and making more noise than anyone. At times, this means you need to be a little bit fanatical, to be the one who seems more excited and enthusiastic than anyone else, and infects others with motivation (remember 'Project the mood' from chapter 7).

Aside from the role you play, let's take a look at three different ways of scaffolding Movement:

» Schedule it in.

» (Re)design the environment.

» Create carrots and sticks.

1. Schedule it in

What does your typical week look like? If you're like most people I work with, the answer is: busy. With so much on our collective plates, there's no guarantee we'll ever find the time to do even the things we commit to doing. Before we know it, we've got more tasks on our to-do list than time in the day allows.

Dermot Crowley, a leading productivity expert and author of *Smart Work*, talks about the importance of scheduling activities proactively in your calendar or your task list. According to Crowley, if it's not in your schedule, it won't happen. 'Time is the fuel that gets things done. Unless you are putting the resource of time against your priorities, you won't get traction.'[28]

Each time you *talk action* as part of establishing buy-in, schedule that action in. You might say something like, 'Let's pull out our diaries and schedule in the key things that need to happen between now and the next time we get together.' Even better, try to identify a frequency or a pattern of appointments: 'How often should we get together? Let's schedule in the next two sessions now, even if we need to change them down the track.'

When I help teams to develop their strategy, I ensure that quarterly reviews are scheduled in advance. These are an opportunity for the team to regroup and review their progress, and also how they are working together as a team. Putting these in the diary from the outset makes it almost certain the review meetings happen, even if they need to be rescheduled. It also sends a powerful message to the team that they are serious about keeping the day's outcomes alive.

Perhaps not everyone will welcome you trying to muscle in on their schedule, in which case it can be a good idea to simply reach agreement on key milestones instead, and then lock in a time to review progress.

2. (Re)design the environment

Getting up early is not my thing. So when I decided to create a routine of early-morning exercise, setting my alarm for 5.30 am, I found myself doing little more than exercising the snooze button most days of the week. After several months of this, a friend made a simple suggestion: 'Why don't you move your alarm clock so it's at the end of your bed? That way you have to get up to turn it off.' I instantly knew this was a good idea, not just because I'd have to get up, but because I also knew what my wife would do if I tried to crawl back into bed after making all that noise. I implemented the idea the next day, and I've hardly missed an early start since. Sure, it was hard work for the first month or so (and occasionally still is), but after several months of getting up at that time, I now look forward to my early morning jaunt. I've formed the habit. Now getting up early *is* my thing.

Simple environmental tweaks like this are designed to make it hard to revert to old habits, and easy to forge new ones. Chip and Dan Heath write about this idea in their book *Switch: How to Change When Change Is Hard*. As they put it, 'Tweaking the environment is about making the right behaviours a little bit easier and the wrong behaviours a little bit harder.'

CASE STUDY: 'Paper please'

Consider the example of Lena. Lena had been charged with responsibility for reducing paper usage in her office. Knowing that circulating a 'please use less paper' message was unlikely to inspire anyone, Lena thought hard about the *Big So What* of the initiative, and ultimately framed the opportunity to her colleagues as one of reducing the company's environmental impact — tying it back to the company's values of 'caring about the bigger picture'.

Lena did a fabulous job. People responded positively to her campaign, and there was strong commitment from her target audience (which was a large one, as it comprised pretty much everyone in the company). Yet three months later, to Lena's dismay, paper usage hadn't gone down at all. In fact, it had gone up! Lena was dumbstruck. *What more can I do? Everyone seemed so receptive. What's wrong with them?*

Then one of Lena's colleagues made a suggestion, half in jest: why don't you get rid of the paper? At first, Lena thought, *I can't do that, people will kill me.* But after thinking on it for a while, it dawned on her: what did she have to lose? Lena took the paper away from the various printers and photocopiers, leaving only a few reams at each. She sent out an email to everyone in the office, telling them, *In keeping with everyone's pledge to reduce our paper usage, I've taken the plunge and reduced our paper supply. Please use what's there wisely.*

At first some people were incensed, but it didn't take long for everyone to adjust and soon paper usage across the office had dropped significantly. Lena had successfully engineered Movement by redesigning the environment.

3. Create carrots and sticks

Consider the classic 'swear jar': each time you are caught swearing, you have to put a dollar into it. Or the personal reward: *If I complete this chapter by the end of the week, then I can book myself a massage* (now why didn't I think of that one earlier?). These are called carrots and sticks, essentially rewards and punishments.

There is a prevailing view among behavioural scientists that carrots and sticks are of limited use in motivating smart people to do things. They are easily overused, often out of laziness, and there is an increasing volume of research to suggest that they can in fact *impede* creative thinking.

In the context of buy-in, however, carrots and sticks can be used to scaffold a behaviour that people have already bought into — a kind of retrospective way to keep people on the chosen path. Say, for example, I've bought into the idea that I want to spend more time setting clear goals with the rest of my team. I might first schedule it in by setting up a rhythm of monthly meetings with each member of the team. Then, to help keep me honest, I might create a carrot/stick system. Perhaps I will say to my team, 'If I postpone a meeting, I owe you lunch. If we stick to all of our meetings for the first three months, everyone gets movie tickets.' With this kind of scaffolding in place, I'm guessing I'll think twice before calling out, 'Can we reschedule?'

One group I work with has imposed an automatic penalty on themselves that kicks in when they miss their agreed actions — $50 is taken off the kitchen supplies budget for the following week, and the money instead goes towards charity. Nothing like the fear of not having chocolate biscuits or coffee in the kitchen to keep up motivation!

THE KEY IS TO AVOID *IMPOSING* CONSEQUENCES ON PEOPLE – TO DO SO WOULD BE INCONGRUENT WITH THE FOCUS ON AUTONOMY THROUGHOUT THE PROCESS OF BUILDING BUY-IN.

Carrots and sticks are more effective when they are self-imposed, once the particular course of action or behaviour you're trying to scaffold has already been agreed.

SUSTAIN

So you've successfully managed to get people to Start — to take the all-important first steps needed to get progress happening. In many cases, you will also have needed to Scaffold those actions, helping your target audience maintain a steady course for the first phase of implementing or embedding the change.

As you stand and look towards the horizon, you may now be asking yourself: what happens beyond that first phase? The first, say, 90 days? How do you keep momentum going when people have other new ideas to play with and new rabbit holes to scamper down?

Of course, not all projects, products or initiatives will involve this kind of sustained focus. But if yours does, there are some real risks that are likely to impede long-term traction. People will get bored or distracted. The business will turn its attention elsewhere and new projects will compete for people's time and energy. Staff will come and go, changing the make-up of your stakeholder group. And that's just to name a few of the risks at play.

Let's look at three ways you can keep the momentum going:

» Make progress your focus.

» Create a guild of greatness.

» Ditch it!

1. Make progress your focus

The research is in: people get their mojo from a sense of progress. Even more so than from the kinds of factors managers mistakenly assume to be more important, such as incentives and recognition.[29]

According to motivation expert Dr Jason Fox, author of *The Game Changer*, 'When we can see how our effort is making a difference and contributing to progress, we're more likely to continue to invest effort into the work ... We want to ensure that we invest the finite amount of energy we have each day in something meaningful. Something that is going to contribute to progress towards somewhere or something better.'[30]

THE BIGGER A PROJECT, OR THE LONGER YOU WANT PEOPLE TO ADOPT A PARTICULAR TYPE OF BEHAVIOUR, THE EASIER IT BECOMES TO LOSE SIGHT OF PROGRESS. A LITTLE LIKE CROSSING A VAST OCEAN WITHOUT BEING ABLE TO SEE THE NEAREST SHORE.

And that can sap people of their focus and energy. Which makes it even more important to explore ways in which you can make progress your focus.

To counter this, why not create a highly visible dashboard to track progress? The dashboard might feature pie charts, bar graphs or nice clear percentage ratings — all of which can be helpful. In doing this, it's important to track progress not just in terms of the overall, long-term objectives, but also keeping a clear eye on the *tiny chunks* we looked at under scaffolding. It's useful to give people things they can realistically tick off each week or a similarly short period.

Of course, a dashboard doesn't need to be a fancy electronic thing. In fact, low-tech is often best because it usually means 'hands on'. Take the example of one team I work with who use a wall of flipcharts, each headed with the different stages of their project. Taking inspiration from a workflow management methodology called 'Kanban', each of the flipcharts is headed 'To do', 'Doing now', 'Under review', 'Ready for launch', 'Done' and 'Abandoned'. The team uses index cards to track different components of their project, and each card has the initials of the responsible team member on it. This system really comes to life when the team gathers at the wall to review project status, as each team member takes it in turns to move their cards to the relevant flipchart. This is more than just a task management list — the act of physically moving the different project cards from one flipchart to another is what really brings the sense of progress to life.

IN MAKING PROGRESS YOUR FOCUS, IT'S IMPORTANT TO TRACK MORE THAN JUST THE OBVIOUS METRICS SUCH AS KEY MILESTONES AND DELIVERABLES.

When it comes to the long-term 'health' of a change, think of what other factors indicate positive progress. Shared learning, team morale, customer feedback, number of tried-and-failed experiments ... these might all be equally important things to follow.

2. Create a guild of greatness

A 'community of practice' is a group of people who identify with one another as having a shared interest or passion (perhaps in a way of working, or maintaining a particular philosophy, or sustaining a change), a shared commitment to learning and a shared desire for excellence.

There's nothing new about communities of practice. It's just a cute way to describe any group of people who regularly get together to maintain and improve standards of practice in a given area.

As explained by leading experts in the field Etienne and Beverly Wenger-Trayner, 'In pursuing their interest in their domain, members engage in joint activities and discussions, help each other, and share information. They build relationships that enable them to learn from each other; they care about their standing with each other.'[31]

The beauty of communities of practice is that they take ownership of ensuring excellence in a particular function, project or domain of an organisation. They take the weight of ensuring continuing action off your shoulders, sharing it among the group.

While 'communities of practice' is generally used to describe groups that are focused on excellence across an entire domain (such as engineering, product design or software coding), the concept can also be used to harness the way people engage around any long-term project or initiative.

If the change matters enough, and enough people care, then there's an opportunity to foster something akin to a community of practice.

WHAT'S MORE, THE VERY NATURE OF BUILDING BUY-IN *LENDS* ITSELF TO THE CREATION OF A COMMUNITY OF PRACTICE.

After all the effort you've put into creating a group of people who are genuinely motivated to act on an idea or initiative, and who are themselves catalysts, what better platform for establishing a 'guild of greatness'.

The topic of building communities of practice is way more involved than we can go into here. A great place to start is understanding what it means to start a movement. Watch Derek Siver's much-loved TED talk[32] for more, or read Seth Godin's *Tribes* or Etienne Wenger, Richard McDermott and William M. Snyder's *Cultivating Communities of Practice*.

3. Ditch it!

Okay, I don't mean you should actually ditch your idea, but you should be *willing* to do so or at least change direction. After all, there's an important difference between sustaining movement and flogging a dead horse. Save your energy (and everyone else's) for the things that really matter.

Eric Ries, the author of *The Lean Start-Up*, talks about the need for companies to regularly take an honest look at the things they're working on and to make a decision whether to 'Pivot' (change course) or 'Persevere' (keep going). I've also heard people add a third option: 'Perish', which involves ditching the project or product and focusing your efforts elsewhere.

It's so easy to become stuck persevering for too long with an idea.

WE HAVE A TENDENCY TO BECOME OVER-INVESTED IN OUR OWN EFFORTS TO THE POINT WHERE WE MAKE IRRATIONAL DECISIONS TO PERSIST. THIS IS WHAT PSYCHOLOGISTS CALL *SUNK COST FALLACY*.

To avoid falling into the trap, step back from your initiative at least once every 90 days, and ask yourself: do I need to pivot, persevere or (perish the thought) perish?

Over to you

Think of an idea or initiative you're working on now. How can you ensure that you convert your target audience's agreement into action?

Start. How will you get those critical first steps to happen?

Scaffold. What will you do to ensure that there is enough support and infrastructure in place to keep people on the right path?

Sustain. How will you create action or change that lasts beyond everyone's initial enthusiasm?

* * *

In this chapter we took people's willing hearts and minds and converted their buy-in to action. Congratulations, you've taken those first steps on Lao Tzu's thousand-mile journey. So, I hear you ask, what now? Great question. What *are* you going to do now? Let me give you something to think about, as we draw this book to a close.

Roadmap for buy-in

Summarising the journey

We began this book with a simple question: how do you *get heard* and *get results*? We've answered this by exploring what it takes to engage people and generate their buy-in to your ideas and initiatives.

In Part I, we examined how you *Get Ready* for buy-in. After all, you wouldn't get onto an aeroplane to go skydiving without first assessing the conditions and checking your parachute, right?

The process of buy-in requires that you do ample preparation before you get going:

» **SHIFT:** Understand and choose the real power of buy-in (chapter 1).

» **MINDSET:** Prep your mindset to become a champion of buy-in (chapter 2).

» **CONVICTION:** Create conviction; step into the role of *catalyst* (chapter 3).

» **WHO:** Identify the social landscape and *choose your who's* (chapter 4).

» **TIMING:** Read the play; assess the prevailing conditions and adjust your approach (chapter 5).

» **YOU:** Think carefully about what you're projecting to your audience (chapter 6).

With these foundations in place, in Part II we moved from *Get Ready* to **Go.**

You learned to engage your target audience across the three dimensions of the 3M model:

» **MOOD:** Make your target audience feel like saying yes (chapter 7).

» **MIND:** Give them a reason to say yes, but go slow to go fast (chapter 8).

» **MOVEMENT:** Talk action and accountability to ensure agreement turns into action (chapter 9).

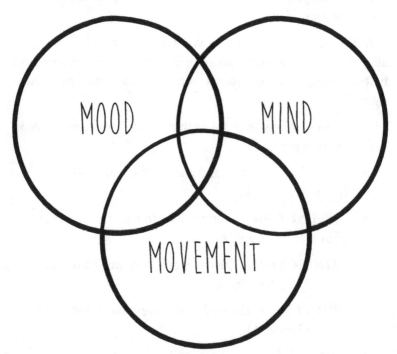

Treat this book as your personal GPS. Use it to help you decide the route you want to take, but also come back to it when you feel you've drifted off track and need some guidance. Start with one map, and reroute when necessary.

As you do so, remember this gem from Albert Einstein: 'Logic will get you from A to Z; imagination will get you everywhere.' As much as it's been my aim to break the gentle art of buy-in into a set of practical stages, when it comes down to it, it's not a step-by-step process in the pure sense.

Buy-in is a *human* challenge. In essence it revolves around people and, let's face it, people can be unpredictable. So, as you follow the map, look for the magic that lies in the side streets and the crazy detours. Listen to your audience, observe them and ask yourself, 'What do they really need in this moment?' Engage in the conversation. Follow your gut.

Most importantly, remember to have fun!

Where to now?

'When you're finished changing, you're finished.'
Benjamin Franklin

'An ounce of practice is worth more than tons of preaching.'
Mahatma Gandhi

Given that we just spent the whole of chapter 9 on Movement, I couldn't let you put this book down without first *talking action*.

This is the point where you ask yourself: What can I do to make sure I put the ideas from this book to good use? Here are four simple suggestions to get you going:

Start small

Pick just one idea from this book, and identify a low-risk situation in which you can give it a go. Maybe you'd like to play with the three perception dials from chapter 6. Or perhaps you'll pick one of the Mood strategies from chapter 7. Whatever you choose, it is only the first step in implementing the ideas in this book. Treat it as a learning experiment. After you've tried it, step back and review how it went. What did you learn from it? What went well? What will you do differently next time?

Make yourself accountable

Create some scaffolding by setting one or two goals and talking accountability with your manager or a mentor. For example, you might set a goal of 'Draw on the Mood strategies in each presentation I do to our key accounts next month' or 'Identify ways of scaffolding any workflow changes agreed with the product development team'. Make those goals visible. Include them on the agenda every time you catch up with your manager — and ask them to be your coach. (You could even discreetly leave a copy of this book on their desk.)

Work as a team

If you haven't already completed the 'Over to you' section at the end of each chapter, now is a great time to do so. Use those exercises as discussion points for your team or a group of friends or colleagues, and work through some of them together. Draw on the ideas in this book to build a shared language among your team. Imagine how powerful it would be if you could all talk easily about the challenges of building buy-in and offer each other support. Before you know it, you'll have created your own culture of buy-in.

'Lean in' to the discomfort

When you put on a new pair of shoes, they often feel stiff and uncomfortable, as if they don't really belong to you. It's the same when trying anything new. The first few times will feel unusual. The words won't feel natural. Or you may feel as though you're getting it all wrong. That's normal — in fact, it's a sign that you're challenging yourself to grow. Reading this book won't make you instantly fluent in the language of buy-in. The only thing that can get you to that place is practice and repetition, and being prepared to make a few mistakes along the way. As world champion basketball player Michael Jordan so wonderfully put it: 'I've missed more than 9000 shots in my career. I've lost almost 300 games. 26 times, I've been trusted to take the game winning shot and missed. I've failed over and over and over again in my life. And that is why I succeed.'

Epilogue

'Coming together is a beginning; keeping together is progress;
working together is success.'

Henry Ford

Not long ago I was speaking at a conference of educators about some of the ideas in this book. Generating buy-in was important to them because a big part of their role is to influence the way their schools adapt to be more inclusive of students with different learning needs. At the lunch break, right after my presentation, one of the audience members came over to me — plate of sandwiches in hand — and said, 'It's funny, you know, there are so many of us here celebrating the work that we do, feeling inspired by the stories we're sharing with each other; but at the end of the day, if we can't get our teachers, parents and students on board, then our impact is constrained by the number of people in this room.'

That one comment pretty much sums up why I embarked on this project. Ultimately, this book is about tapping into the power of collaboration — the single most important capability for any organisation seeking to thrive in a world that's changing faster than ever. A culture of buy-in is the rocket fuel of collaboration.

In collaborative cultures, great ideas don't sit idly gathering dust, nor do they fall through cracks in the social landscape. Important projects and initiatives don't fail for a lack of cooperation. People don't become frustrated and disengaged because of conflicting opinions coming at them from managers who themselves don't seem to be on the same page.

Organisational politics don't cause inertia and confusion. The customer is never forgotten.

Truly collaborative teams and organisations are a force to be reckoned with. In the face of all the change that's happening around us, these are the organisations that are able to read the play and adapt the fastest. To *lead* change, even. This is their *collaborative edge*.

But hey, you already know that ... because you're a champion of buy-in, right?

Notes

1. www.theaustralian.com.au/business/aviation/m-qantas-parts-system-flop/story-e6frg95x-1111113142401

2. Sometimes referred to as the 'quarternary' sector of the economy (as opposed to tertiary or secondary), this is now the biggest source of revenue and employment in the Western economies.

3. Interview with David Noël published in *First Round Review*, http://firstround.com/review/how-soundcloud-keeps-communication-flowing-across-4-offices-in-4-time-zones/

4. According to Richard Gesteland, author of *Cross-Cultural Business Behaviour: A Guide for Global Management*, most countries in Asia, Europe and Latin America operate to a formal, hierarchical norm.

5. http://istart.com.au/feature-article/switched-on-cfo-peter-gregg-qantas/

6. http://blog.foundersmentality.com/2014/08/05/going-slow-to-go-fast/

7. See hbr.org/2014/07/the-stakeholders-you-need-to-close-a-big-deal/. In this article, Weinstein uses the term 'champions' rather than the term 'allies'. I've omitted that language to avoid confusion with my own term from chapter 2, *champion of buy-in* — a different concept.

8. I use the term *target audience* throughout this book to describe the stakeholders you've targeted to engage with in your quest to build buy-in. While the word 'audience' might evoke an image of rows of people sitting in an auditorium, I mean it much more broadly than that. If I am sitting in a meeting with you, and I'm seeking your buy-in, then you are my audience.

9. Malcolm Gladwell (2002), *The Tipping Point: How Little Things Can Make a Big Difference.*

10. I've changed Tim's name to respect his privacy. I've done this with most of my own examples in this book.

11. Cuddy, A. J., Fiske, S. T., & Glick, P. (2008). Warmth and competence as universal dimensions of social perception: The stereotype content model and the BIAS map. *Advances in experimental social psychology, 40,* 61–149.

12. Stephen R. Covey (2007 [1989]), *The 7 Habits of Highly Effective People.*

13. www.nytimes.com/2015/08/06/opinion/america-deserves-a-servant-leader.html

14. Antonio Damasio (2005), *Descartes' Error: Emotion, Reason and the Human Brain.* Damasio found that patients with damaged emotional function were unable even to make decisions.

15. J. A. Russell (1980). A Circumplex Model of Affect. *Journal of Personality and Social Psychology, 39,* 1161–78.

16. Gabrielle Dolan (2017), *Stories for Work: The essential guide to business storytelling.* The quote here was shared with me in an interview.

17. https://www.youtube.com/watch?v=qfv6Ah_MVJU

18. The UK and Japanese versions of the ads were recast with local actors.

19. To see this video, simply Google 'Jamie Oliver TED talk'.

20. In *Chapters from My Autobiography*, Twain attributed this quote to British prime minister Benjamin Disraeli, although it's debatable whether Disraeli ever said it. There's simply no proof, and I don't propose to lie — especially in this section of the book. Hopefully we can agree on one thing, though: it's a cool quote. 'Lies, damned lies and statistics' was also the title of an episode of *The West Wing*.

21. www.cmo.com.au/article/586585/five-lessons-from-expedia-test-and-learn-culture/

22. www.abc.net.au/news/2015-12-12/world-adopts-climate-deal-at-paris-talks/7023712

23. This is an oft-heard distortion of Benjamin Franklin's more dignified advice, 'Don't put off until tomorrow what you can do today.'

24. Danny Ertel (2004), 'Getting Past Yes: Negotiating as if Implementation Mattered', *Harvard Business Review*, November.

25. I use an app called Countdown MiniTimer. It's brilliant.

26. www.theage.com.au/news/national/on-track-for-record-low-road-toll/2006/08/27/1156617212517.html

27. www.atlassian.com/company/shipit

28. Shared with me in an interview with Crowley.

29. In 2010, Teresa M. Amabile and Steven J. Kramer published a breakthrough study in the *Harvard Business Review*. https://hbr.org/2010/01/the-hbr-list-breakthrough-ideas-for-2010

30. Jason Fox (2014). *The Game Changer: How to Use the Science of Motivation with the Power of Game Design to Shift Behaviour, Shape Culture and Make Clever Happen*, page 82.

31. From 'Communities of Practice: A Brief Introduction', http://wenger-trayner.com/introduction-to-communities-of-practice/

32. https://www.ted.com/talks/derek_sivers_how_to_start_a_movement